32

EYE ON ART

The Great Surrealists
Dreamers and Artists

By Vanessa Oswald

Portions of this book originally appeared in *Surrealism* by Hal Marcovitz.

LUCENT
PRESS

Published in 2019 by
Lucent Press, an Imprint of Greenhaven Publishing, LLC
353 3rd Avenue
Suite 255
New York, NY 10010

Designer: Deanna Paternostro
Editor: Vanessa Oswald   APR 3 0 2019

Library of Congress Cataloging-in-Publication Data

Names: Oswald, Vanessa, author.
Title: The great surrealists : dreamers and artists / Vanessa Oswald.
Description: New York : Lucent Press, 2019. | Series: Eye on art | Includes
    bibliographical references and index.
Identifiers: LCCN 2018027539 (print) | LCCN 2018029118 (ebook) | ISBN
    9781534566064 (eBook) | ISBN 9781534566057 (library bound book) | ISBN
    9781534566040 (pbk. book)
Subjects: LCSH: Surrealism–Juvenile literature.
Classification: LCC N6494.S8 (ebook) | LCC N6494.S8 O89 2019 (print) | DDC
    700/.41163–dc23
LC record available at https://lccn.loc.gov/2018027539

Printed in the United States of America

CPSIA compliance information: Batch #BW19KL: For further information contact Greenhaven Publishing LLC, New York, New York at 1-844-317-7404.

Please visit our website, www.greenhavenpublishing.com. For a free color catalog of all our high-quality
books, call toll free 1-844-317-7404 or fax 1-844-317-7405.

Contents

Foreword

What is art? There is no one answer to that question. Every person has a different idea of what makes something a work of art. Some people think of art as the work of masters such as Leonardo da Vinci, Mary Cassatt, or Michelangelo. Others see artistic beauty in everything from skyscrapers and animated films to fashion shows and graffiti. Everyone brings their own point of view to their interpretation of art.

Discovering the hard work and pure talent behind artistic techniques from different periods in history and different places around the world helps people develop an appreciation for art in all its varied forms. The stories behind great works of art and the artists who created them have fascinated people for many years and continue to do so today. Whether a person has a passion for painting, graphic design, or another creative pursuit, learning about the lives of great artists and the paths that can be taken to achieve success as an artist in the modern world can inspire budding creators to pursue their dreams.

This series introduces readers to different artistic styles, as well as the artists who made those styles famous. As they read about creative expression in the past and present, they are challenged to think critically about their own definition of art.

Quotes from artists, art historians, and other experts provide a unique perspective on each topic, and a detailed bibliography is provided as a starting place for further research. In addition, a list of websites and books about each topic encourages readers to continue their exploration of the fascinating world of art.

This world comes alive with each turn of the page, as readers explore sidebars about the artistic process and creative careers. Essential examples of different artistic styles are presented in the form of vibrant photographs and historical images, giving readers a comprehensive look at art history from ancient times to the present.

Art may be difficult to define, but it is easy to appreciate. In developing a deeper understanding of different art forms, readers will be able to look at the world around them with a fresh perspective on the beauty that can be found in unexpected places.

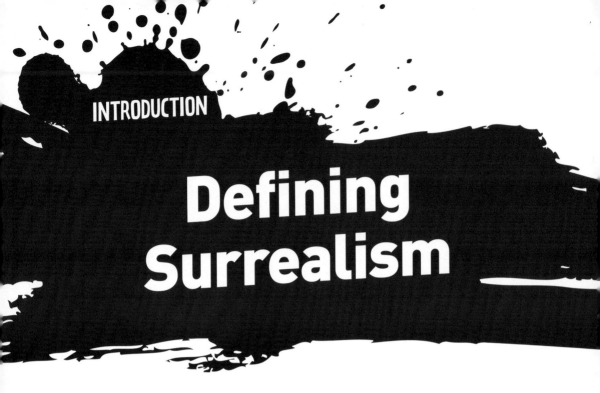

Defining Surrealism

A man with his long nose fit perfectly into a pipe, a lobster telephone, a pair of boots that turn into feet, and a fish with a woman's legs on the beach: These are some of the most familiar images in Surrealism, a movement in modern art that hit its peak just under a century ago. The Surrealist images painted by such artists as Salvador Dalí, René Magritte, Max Ernst, Joan Miró, André Masson, Man Ray, and others have continued to startle, bewilder, and fascinate art lovers for decades.

Today, Surrealism knows no boundaries, and the movement's impact can be recognized in various artistic outlets. Contemporary artists, who are inspired by the early Surrealists, have learned from the foundational elements of Surrealism. They have absorbed this knowledge, allowing it to transform their own work to speak on behalf of their own unusual ideas. As a result, they create their own brands of Surrealist art, and just like their predecessors, with these new ideas and exciting artistry, they too will inspire future generations.

Apollinaire and Freud

"Surrealism" is a word coined in 1917 by the French poet Guillaume Apollinaire to describe a production of the ballet *Parade*. The ballet's producers had asked Apollinaire to write the text that appeared in the programs handed to audience members. It fell upon his shoulders to prepare the unsuspecting ballet lovers for the unusual performance that awaited them.

The ballet featured set designs and costumes by Spanish artist Pablo Picasso and the music of French composer Erik Satie. The ballet was light and whimsical, telling the story of circus performers and featuring jazzy music that was made by such unusual "instruments" as a typewriter, siren, pistol, and foghorn. The costumes and set designs were hardly what anyone would expect to see on the ballet stage. Some of the costumes were made of cardboard, while the set designs, which depicted a 19th century street carnival, reflected Picasso's interest in abstract art. To sum up this odd combination of the real and unreal, Apollinaire described the ballet as *surréalisme* or, in English, "super realism."

Surrealism describes an image in which the unusual is depicted as a part of everyday life. However, true Surrealism involves much more than just a visual image.

Surrealists were heavily influenced by Sigmund Freud, the founder of psychoanalysis, who suggested that

Guillaume Apollinaire created the word "Surrealism" to describe Jean Cocteau's ballet Parade.

Sigmund Freud influenced the views of many Surrealists.

humans are driven more by subconscious (something that is in the part of the mind that a person is not aware of) thoughts than conscious thoughts. Psychoanalysts such as Freud and Carl Jung suggested that the subconscious is a dark place that harbors inner drives, demons, frustrations, fears, and obsessions. Further, Jung believed that some universal thoughts are shared by all human minds, which explains how societies and cultures far removed from one another develop similar beliefs, rituals, and symbols. Jung suggested the subconscious holds the key to linking all human thought. In addition, Freud and Jung believed the subconscious remains active during sleep, manifesting itself in the form of dreams that often contain symbols. For example, a man who dreams his house has been robbed may, in his waking hours, be stealing from someone else. Perhaps his thefts are real; for example, he may be helping himself to the cash register at his place of employment. Maybe his thefts are not quite as obvious; for example, he may be taking a longer lunch at work. Nevertheless, in his subconscious mind, he believes he is stealing from his employer. His shame has manifested itself in the form of a dream in which he is the victim of a theft. In his 1900 book *The Interpretation of Dreams*, Freud said, "If I dream I am frightened of robbers, the robbers are certainly imaginary, but the fear is real."[1]

Uncovering the Subconscious

Surrealists strive to tap their subconscious to create art; however, subconscious thoughts are not easily found. After all, they do not appear in an artist's brain at will. Surrealists believe subconscious thoughts make themselves apparent during dreams or through "automatism," or free association, which was also a concept explored by Freud. To free-associate, a Surrealist may observe a scene and then immediately apply the next thought that enters their mind to that image.

Jennifer Mundy, former senior curator at the Tate Gallery in London, England, said Freud helped the Surrealists realize that they did not have to limit themselves to painting landscapes, portraits, and still life images that artists had been painting for centuries. Mundy wrote,

> The surrealists took from Freud confirmation of the existence of a deep reservoir of unknown and scarcely tapped energies within the psyche. Their use of techniques to reduce the element of conscious control in their drawings and writings, and their patient recording of dream imagery were more and more seen by theorists of the movement as attempts to express the inner world of undirected and uncensored thought that Freud had described.[2]

Indeed, Freud once said, "The *interpretation* of dreams is the royal road to a *knowledge* of the unconscious *activities* of the mind."[3] Surrealists regarded that statement as a challenge to explore their dreams and free associations and create an outlet for their interpretations.

Fusion of Real and Make-Believe

Once they made it onto canvas, images from those dreams and free associations took on many strange shapes, colors, and concepts. Examples of Surrealist art include *The Man in the Bowler Hat*, painted by Magritte, depicting a man wearing a bowler hat with his face obscured by a white dove flying by and a painting by Ernst titled *The Elephant Celebes*, which depicts a green mechanical elephant with the head of a bull. However, one of the most famous Surrealist images ever painted is *The Persistence of Memory* by Dalí, which depicts the faces of watches melting in an empty, desertlike landscape.

All these images certainly depict unusual and even inexplicable events occurring in what are otherwise familiar scenes of human existence. What makes them truly Surrealist is the artist's ability to explore the depths of their subconscious and transfer those thoughts to the canvas. By creating a Surrealist image, the artist hopes to convey the universal experience of humankind in a symbolic way.

When the early Surrealists first began producing artwork, their pieces were not as readily appreciated as they are today; some of these artists only received significant recognition after their deaths. Current artists who produce Surrealist art, who have been deeply inspired by early Surrealists, create in several different art forms: painting, photography, art installations, collage, sculpture, dance, writing, digital art, and more. While the future of art is unknown, artists will surely keep creating without limitations as a tribute to Surrealism, continuing to fascinate art lovers for ages.

CHAPTER ONE

Early Surrealism

After the devastation of World War I in Europe, a diverse group of artists and intellectuals gathered in places such as coffee shops in Paris, France, to try to make sense of the chaos. Through these meetings, the Surrealist school of art was born. Their ideas were unconventional and their art was vastly different when compared to art made by traditional artists during this era.

Poet André Breton was typically the person at the center of these discussions, providing the most influence on the early Surrealist artists. Breton, who worked in a French mental hospital during the war, had studied Freud and wondered whether the subconscious could be tapped as a source for literature. At first, Breton was skeptical that the visual arts could become an outlet for Surrealism, but when artists joined his movement and started producing works drawn from their subconscious thoughts, Breton became an advocate of the genre.

Many of the early Surrealist artists had been working in other genres, including the abstract styles known as Dadaism and Cubism, both of which would influence Surrealism. The early Surrealists experimented with their styles, refining their work to fit into the rules of Surrealism that Breton recorded in a manifesto he published in 1924. For much of the decade of the 1920s, Surrealist art would be confined to the galleries of Paris. However, late in the decade, Salvador Dalí joined the movement and helped spread Surrealism to an international audience.

Inspirational Art Forms

During World War I, Dadaism emerged in Switzerland and soon spread throughout the European continent. (The French word *dada* means "hobby-horse." It was a whimsical expression picked for the name of the genre of art by two of its founders, Hugo Ball and Richard Huelsenbeck.) Like the Surrealists, the Dadaists incorporated unusual images into otherwise ordinary scenes. For example, French Dadaist Marcel Duchamp mocked Leonardo da Vinci's masterpiece, the *Mona Lisa*, by painting a mustache and beard on the woman in the picture. Another early Duchamp work depicts an upside-down men's room urinal. "Dada is the ground from which all art springs," French Dadaist Jean Arp said. "Dada stands for art without sense. This does not mean nonsense. Dada is without a meaning, as Nature is."[4] As Arp's words show, the Dadaists had a generally comical outlook on life, and their art was certainly not drawn from any subconscious source. Still, Surrealism owes something of a debt to Dadaism, because the Dadaists showed that art did not have to be limited to portraits, landscapes, still life scenes, and other familiar images but could be based on whatever ideas an artist might have.

Another art form that would provide inspiration for Surrealism is Cubism. In Cubism the artist dissects an image, breaks it down into tiny pieces, and then reassembles the images in an abstract form. Cubist portraits, such as those made by Picasso, often show hands, ears, heads, arms, and legs depicted out of place. When other objects are included in the scene, the painter is practicing a form of Cubism known as Synthetic Cubism or Collage Cubism, after the French word for "paste-up." (Synthetic Cubists often paste other materials—scraps of newspaper, swatches of cloth, discarded railroad tickets, or trash from the wastepaper basket—right onto the canvas.) The artist given the most credit for developing Synthetic Cubism is Frenchman Georges Braque, whose 1913 painting *Still Life with Playing Cards* is regarded as a prime example of the genre. In the painting are drawings of cards from a deck as well as other images, such as a bunch of grapes, broken down into their most basic geometric shapes. Braque also included wood grains and other textures in the painting. Alfred H. Barr Jr., former director of the Museum of Modern Art (MoMA) in New York, wrote,

> In the Still Life with Playing Cards the geometrical shapes are so remotely related to the original form of the object that they seem almost to have been invented rather than derived. Their texture further adds to their independent reality so they may be considered not a breaking down or analysis, but a building up or synthesis.[5]

Later, some Surrealists would adopt the techniques of the Cubists, breaking

Marcel Duchamp is one of the most recognizable artists of the Dadaist movement.

Marcel Duchamp's Influence

The work of French Dadaist Duchamp heavily influenced the early Surrealists. Born into a family of artists in the French village of Blainville-Crevon in 1887, Duchamp drew and painted in the classical style before embracing abstract art styles, such as Cubism.

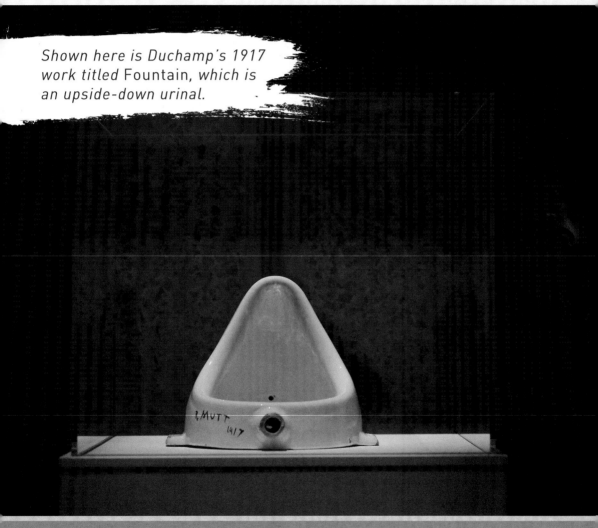

Shown here is Duchamp's 1917 work titled Fountain, *which is an upside-down urinal.*

1. "Marcel Duchamp: Fountain," Tate, www.tate.org.uk/art/artworks/duchamp-fountain-t07573.
2. Quoted in Hector Obalk, "The Unfindable Readymade," Tout-Fait, May 2000. www.toutfait.com/issues/issue_2/Articles/obalk.html.
3. Quoted in Obalk, "The Unfindable Readymade."

He painted his most famous Cubist work, *Nude Descending a Staircase, No. 2*, in 1912. Duchamp's work titled *Fountain*, which was a porcelain urinal with the signature "R.Mutt,"[1] was among the works of Dada art he called "readymades,"[2] which was first defined in André Breton and Paul Éluard's *Dictionnaire Abrégé du Surréalisme* as "an ordinary object elevated to the dignity of a work of art by the mere choice of an artist."[3]

Among his other readymades were a snow shovel, titled *In Advance of the Broken Arm*, and *Bicycle Wheel*, which he mounted on a wooden stool. Duchamp created little art in his later years. He became an American citizen in 1955 and died in Paris in 1968.

down objects and rearranging them into new shapes on the canvas or drawing in completely unassociated objects as part of the image.

Principles of Surrealism

Some of the artists had to take a leave from Dadaism and Cubism to fight in World War I. Ernst served in the German army as an artilleryman. Masson, who fought in the French army, sustained a gunshot wound in the chest; the stretcher-bearers were unable to remove him from the battlefield and were forced to leave him behind for the night. Miraculously, he survived. His biographer, Otto Hahn, suggested that Masson, gravely wounded and lying on his back, looked up at the stars and experienced his first Surrealist inspiration. Hahn wrote, "The world around him became something wondrous and he experienced his first complete physical release, while in the sky there appeared before him a torso of light."[6]

Breton also served in World War I. Stationed for a time as a medical orderly in a mental hospital in the French town of Saint Dizier, Breton tended to the soldiers who had experienced psychological trauma on the battlefield. In the hospital, he saw physicians working with the patients, trying to unlock the tormented thoughts from their minds, often through hypnosis. Familiar with Freud's theories, Breton wondered whether subconscious thoughts could be articulated in literature. Later, in describing his experiences at Saint Dizier, Breton said, "The time

André Breton was a pioneer of early Surrealism. He published the Manifesto of Surrealism *in 1924, which highlighted the rules of the unique art movement.*

I spent in this place, and the attention with which I studied what was happening have counted immensely in my life and have undoubtedly had a decisive influence on my manner of thinking."[7]

After the war, other writers and artists joined Breton in Paris's cafés, where Surrealism was born. In 1920, Breton, with coauthor Philippe Soupault, published the novel *Les Champs Magnétiques* (in English, *The Magnetic Fields*), which is regarded as the first work of Surrealist literature. In writing the book, Breton and Soupault broke numerous literary conventions. For example, they ended chapters at whatever point in the story they happened to be when they quit work for the day. The next morning, they would pick up the story where they left off by starting a new chapter. Breton and Soupault also employed the technique of automatism—they let thoughts spill out of their minds onto the pages of the book, letting one word inspire the next. The fact that their sentences often made no sense did not discourage them from completing their manuscript. One of the book's sentences reads, "Do not disturb the genius planter of white roots my nerve endings underground."[8] While critics debated the value of Surrealist literature, Breton and the other Surrealists pressed on.

In 1924, the rules and concepts of Surrealism were drawn up by Breton, who issued his *Manifesto of Surrealism*. He defined Surrealism as a pure state of psychic automatism, by which a person wants to express the functioning of thought either through the written word, verbally, or through any other form. He further defined Surrealism as dictated by thought without any control exercised by reason, as well as exempt from any concerns, such as beauty or morals. In describing Surrealism, Breton wrote,

> *Surrealism is based on the belief in the superior reality of certain forms of previously neglected associations, in the omnipotence of dream, in the disinterested play of thought. It tends to ruin once and for all all other psychic mechanisms and to substitute itself for them in solving all the principal problems of life.*[9]

Breton intended Surrealism to provide new rules for literature. At first, he rejected visual art as an outlet for Surrealism but eventually came to believe Surrealism could be the basis for any type of artistic expression. In fact, elsewhere in the manifesto, he talked about a dream in which he envisioned a man, who had been sliced in two, standing at his window. Clearly, he appreciated the artistic possibilities inherent in such a vision. Describing the image of the severed man in his dream, Breton wrote,

> *There could be no question of ambiguity, accompanied as it was by the faint visual image ... Were I a painter, this visual depiction*

Breton's Life

P oet and novelist André Breton gave voice to the concept of Surrealism. His *Manifesto of Surrealism* defined the movement and served as a guide for artists, writers, filmmakers, and other creative people who wished to employ Surrealism in their work. Born in the Normandy region of France in 1896, Breton studied to be a physician but turned to writing after serving as a medical orderly in a mental hospital during World War I.

The desk of André Breton was on display at the Henri-Martin Museum in Cahors, France, in 2014.

Breton admired 19th-century French poet Arthur Rimbaud, who was one of the originators of the French symbolist style of literature. To tell their stories, symbolists rely heavily on the use of symbols or metaphors rather than descriptions of real-life objects and experiences. Artists eventually adopted the use of symbolist concepts as well. Certainly, the Surrealists were inspired by the symbolist movement.

Breton was also influenced by the writings of Karl Marx. He embraced Socialism and encouraged other surrealists to adopt Socialism as well, and many of them did follow Breton into the movement. Breton joined the French Communist party in 1927. In World War II, he served in the French army but was expelled by the Nazi-backed Vichy government for his Socialist activism. He fled to the United States and Canada, but after the war, he returned to Paris, where he continued to support Socialism and also made efforts to revive the Surrealist movement. He died in 1966.

would doubtless have become more important for me ... Since that day, I have had occasion to concentrate my attention voluntarily on similar apparitions, and I know they are fully as clear as auditory phenomena. With a pencil and white sheet of paper to hand, I could easily trace their outlines.[10]

Parisian Art Reaches New Heights

It did not take long for artists to be drawn to the Surrealist movement. In 1925, the first major exhibition of Surrealist art was displayed at the Galerie Pierre in Paris, which featured the work of Masson, Miró, and Man Ray, an artist-photographer whose real name was Emmanuel Radnitzky. Born in Philadelphia, Pennsylvania, Ray first experimented with Dadaism after meeting Duchamp in New York; in 1921, he moved to Paris and embraced Surrealism. Ray was mostly a painter, but he would soon experiment with photography. In 1926, Galerie Surréaliste, a gallery in Paris devoted to Surrealism, opened with an exhibition of Ray's art.

This was an exciting time to be an artist in Paris. Following the war, creative people from many walks of life converged on the French capital, taking up residence in the cultured district known as the Left Bank. Many were American writers, including Ernest Hemingway,

In the 1920s, artists of all kinds flocked to the cafés of Paris to talk about art.

Gertrude Stein, Ezra Pound, and F. Scott Fitzgerald. They spent their afternoons in cafés or in each other's tiny flats, playing cards, sipping wine, and discussing art, jazz, literature, and politics. In the evenings, the Left Bank dwellers made the rounds of the city's bistros. In between the drinking, card-playing, and leisurely strolls along the Champs-Elysées, books were written, music was composed, and paintings were created. Indeed, all the arts were heading in new directions. The Surrealists were a part of this community, and there is no question that they were among the most creative artists to emerge from Paris in the 1920s.

The early paintings by the Surrealists show how they absorbed Breton's pronouncements about Surrealism and adopted it into their work. Ernst painted *The Elephant Celebes* in 1921, featuring an elephant against a desertlike background—with a few fish swimming across the sky—while a headless naked woman bids the elephant to follow her. Art historian Uwe M. Schneede suggested that *The Elephant Celebes* is a clear example of how Surrealists aimed to merge the unreal with the real. Schneede said the objects in the picture are unreal, but Ernst painted them with such clarity and precision that the impression he leaves is one of imaginary objects existing in the real world. Schneede wrote, "In the artificial world of the picture, things that do not exist elsewhere become real. The picture constitutes an anti-world of fantasy and the psychic implications of such a world."[11]

Masson's early Surrealist work employed elements of Cubism. The artist's *Figure in the Underground*, painted in 1924, shows a bald-headed nude unfurling a scroll. In the background are vague representations of a bird, the sun, a bottle on a shelf, and an hourglass. He used few colors in his early Surrealist paintings, preferring to give the images a flat, muted look of grays and subtle red and purple tones. Author Tim Martin said the painting helped lay the groundwork for Masson's later work because it was one of his first paintings to employ symbolism, in which Masson used simple objects to represent much more complex thoughts. In the painting, Martin said, man dominates the objects depicted by Masson, just as he dominates his own universe. He wrote, "Elements of symbolism make this work an important stage in the formation of Masson's more wholly Surrealist paintings."[12]

Miró's 1924 painting *The Gentleman* depicts a very colorful foot providing the lone support for a stick figure that sports a mustache and a shock of red hair that resembles the feathers of a rooster. The figure is painted on a green background. According to the late Carolyn Lanchner, former curator of paintings and sculpture at the MoMA in New York, *The Gentleman* represents a blurring of the lines between the real and the musings of Miró's subconscious. "Miró's fancifully outfitted gentleman delivers poetry by way of humor," Lanchner wrote. "Whatever the picture's source may have been, a fluid ambivalence between physical and mental events is realized."[13]

The Gentleman, like most of Miró's work, was a product of automatism. "I do not start with the idea that I will paint a certain thing," Miró insisted. "I start to paint and while I am painting the picture begins to take effect, it reveals itself. In the act of painting, a shape will begin to mean woman, or bird."[14]

Surrealism Goes Global

The late 1920s marked a major explosion in Surrealist art. In the beginning, the movement had been limited to the Parisian galleries, but by the later years of the decade, artists from other countries had been drawn to the movement, and soon Surrealist art would receive international exposure. As new artists started exploring Surrealism, they brought distinctive styles to the craft. For example, Magritte, a Belgian, painted one of his first Surrealist images, *Le Jockey Perdu* (in English, *The Lost Jockey*), in 1926. The painting depicts a man riding a horse through a landscape of trees that resemble marble columns decorated with bars of music; in the foreground, curtains are drawn back to reveal the scene. A. M. Hammacher, the late

German art critic and former museum director, said Magritte intended the bars of music to dominate the image, hence making the jockey lost in the world of the painting. He wrote, "The bars of music contribute rhythmical transparency to the picture, in which the jockey theme becomes lost as though in some enchanted domain."[15]

Magritte also had a taste for the grotesque. His 1927 painting *The Menaced Assassin* depicts a man listening to a gramophone while a female corpse lies nearby. Standing behind two walls, ready to strike the killer with a club and capture him in a net, are two other men. Meanwhile, three men peer in through a window, standing in front of a background of snow-capped mountains. Evidently, Magritte was influenced by more than his subconscious thoughts. He enjoyed reading detective stories—he even tried writing some himself—and appreciated the dark poetry of Edgar Allan Poe. Schneede said *The Menaced Assassin* represents a technique practiced by many Surrealists—taking a simple story (in this case, a murder) and turning it into a rather elaborate scenario:

> If we accept the picture's invitation to guess at what has gone before and what will happen next, we reach this conclusion: a murderer is spending a moment listening to beautiful music while his captors stand ready to apprehend him. There is no escape, because the window, too, has been blocked. To find so trivial a story worthy of art is typical for a Surrealist.[16]

In addition to Magritte, others drawn to the Surrealist school in Paris were Germans Richard Oelze and Méret Oppenheim, Romanians Victor Brauner and Jacques Hérold, and the Swiss painters Kurt Seligmann and Alberto Giacometti. Also making their way to Paris were Hans Bellmer, a Pole; Wolfgang Paalen, an Austrian; Oscar Dominguez, a Spaniard; Marie Čermínová, a Czech who painted under the name of Toyen; Enrico Donati, an Italian; and Grégoire Michonze, a Russian. Ray remained America's leading Surrealist of the era.

The fact that artists with an interest in Surrealism were flocking to Paris showed how much of an impact the movement had made on the international art community in the handful of years since Breton published his manifesto. Soon the appeal of Surrealism would explode even further, captivating audiences across the globe.

In 1928, Salvador Dalí joined the movement and would be instrumental in turning Surrealism into a major school of art. He was a classically trained painter, although he experimented with a number of abstract styles. Kicked out of art school for his political activism and eccentric behavior but mostly for showing contempt to his teachers—he did not believe them capable of teaching him—he moved to Paris at the urging

Salvador Dalí became one of the most well-known artists of the Surrealist movement.

of Miró, whom he had met in Madrid, Spain. When he arrived, Miró introduced him to the city's most influential Surrealist artists. He was drawn into their circle and soon started painting his own Surrealist images.

Salvador Dalí

Dalí completed his first Surrealist painting, *The First Day of Spring*, in 1929. It provided the benchmark for a career in Surrealism that would span the next five decades. The painting shows a blue sky glistening over a gray landscape populated by various characters—a man sitting in a chair, a little girl confronting an older man, a fish, a nude, a bird's head in a box, a man walking a dog, a baby's picture in a frame, an abstract painting within the painting, an upside-down grasshopper, and other images. The French surrealist community was immediately smitten with his talent. Surrealist poet Robert Desnos said, "It's like nothing that is being done in Paris."[17] As for Dalí, he had no doubt that he belonged in the Surrealist school and, in fact, fully intended to emerge as the leader of the movement. He said,

Although I plunged into the craziest ventures with the same eagerness as they, I was already laying—with Macchiavellian skepticism—the structural foundation for the next step in the eternal tradition. The Surrealists seemed the only ones who formed a group whose methods would serve my plans. Their

leader, André Breton, seemed irreplaceable in his function as visible head of the movement. As for me, I tried to lead, but by means of a secret influence, both opportunistic and contradictory.[18]

Dalí was eccentric. He once gave a lecture at the French university La Sorbonne with his foot submerged in a pail of milk and showed up at a press conference wearing a lobster on his head. When he signed an autograph he always kept the pen. He was also very likely to have suffered from mental illness. He told friends that he feared being devoured alive. Dalí hallucinated and often fell into fits of uncontrollable laughter.

He selected weird and wordy titles for his paintings. Among his wordiest titles was *Skull with Its Lyric Appendage Leaning on a Night Table Which Should Have the Exact Temperature of a Cardinal Bird's Nest*. Nevertheless, his talent was unquestioned. Soon after completing *The First Day of Spring*, he painted *Illumined Pleasures*. The painting featured a variety of human and animal faces, a self-portrait, a pattern of bicyclists, a hand holding a bloody dagger, and a woman splashing waves against a cliff.

In 1931, he painted *The Persistence of Memory*, the painting most responsible for setting the tone for his own work and boosting Surrealism into an international phenomenon. The painting features the faces of watches melting

Salvador Dalí is shown here painting in Spain.

against an empty landscape. The weirdness of *The Persistence of Memory*, along with Dalí's eccentricities, his flamboyance, and his talent at self-promotion, helped catapult Surrealism onto the international stage.

Suddenly, art critics, art collectors, gallery owners, museum curators, and other important people in the art world took notice of this bizarre form of art, which was strange even by abstract standards. Heightened attention was brought to the art genre in 1936 when Dalí was featured on the cover of *TIME* magazine, which used a photo taken by Ray, who was also achieving significant Surrealist milestones at this time. Now Surrealists, such as Dalí and Ray, were being recognized in social circles normally reserved for statesmen, scientists, and sports stars. This excitement surrounding Dalí, along with other celebrated Surrealists of the time, was only the start of the spectacle they shared through their art. Years later, they inspired several artists, helping them tap into their subconscious and unlock the mysteries within their own creative minds.

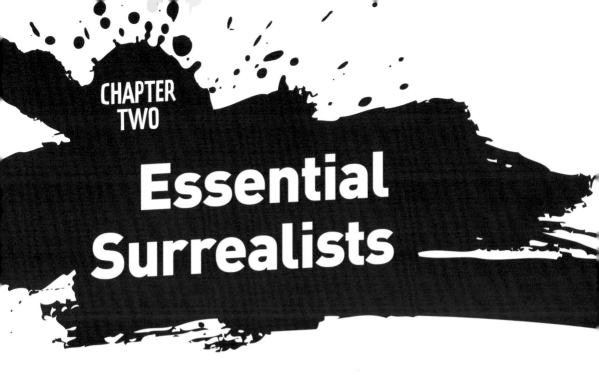

CHAPTER TWO

Essential Surrealists

Each early Surrealist artist had their own claim to fame, and they developed their own preferred methods and techniques for creating art. Most of them found their specific artistic niches through experimentation. All of these unique styles served as important contributions to the genre. Their innovations ranged from tinkering with their paints, canvases, and other materials to much more unusual notions such as starving themselves or depriving themselves of sleep to further probe the secrets of their subconscious thoughts.

The most common theme they maintained in their art, however, was the merger of the real with the unreal, which had been an integral part of Surrealism since the dancers first took the stage in the ballet *Parade*. Dalí had his own term for it. He called it "concrete irrationality."[19] He said,

> *My whole ambition in the pictorial domain is to materialize the images of concrete irrationality … In order that the world of the imagination and of concrete irrationality may be as objectively evident, of the same consistency, of the same durability, of the same persuasive, cognitive and communicable thickness as that of the exterior world of phenomenal reality.*[20]

There is no question that the Surrealists were innovators. Although they took inspiration from the Dadaists, the Cubists, and other abstract artists, their work was unique in many ways.

Serving as the originating members of the school they had founded, the Surrealists set the tone for a style of art that would continue to evolve for years to come.

Dalí's Wife

Many of Dalí's paintings include the image of the same woman. It is his wife, Gala, whom he was married to from 1934 until her death 48 years later.

She was born Elena Ivanovna Diakonova in Russia to wealthy parents. In 1912, at the age of 19, her family sent her to a hospital in Switzerland for treatment of tuberculosis. While undergoing treatment, she met French poet Paul Éluard. Eventually, she married Éluard and moved to Paris with him, where she adopted the name Gala. In 1929, she met Dalí, and soon after, she divorced Éluard to marry the Spanish painter. Dalí was a talented artist, but he knew nothing about business. Gala took over his business affairs, managed his career, and made her husband wealthy.

She died in 1982, seven years before Dalí. He was extremely heartbroken, and for the final years of his life, he lived as a shut-in, meaning he seldom left his house. Suffering from depression and Parkinson's disease, he painted little, starved himself, and withered away until he died. On his deathbed, he made his final Surrealist drawing, titled *Head of Europa*, which he gave to King Juan Carlos of Spain as a gift.

Student of Impressionism

Before embracing Surrealism, Dalí had been trained in the classic style of painting known as Impressionism. Impressionists paint brightly lit images showing vivid colors and broad brush strokes, and they often let their brush strokes bleed over the lines. They were also among the first artists to take their easels outdoors. They believed that painting *en plein air*, a French expression that means "in the open air," gave them the opportunity to capture colors in their most natural forms.

Dalí was born in 1904 in the Spanish town of Figueres in the region of Spain known as Catalonia. Figueres is near Spain's Costa Brava along the Mediterranean Sea. All his life, Dalí was awestruck by the beauty of the Costa Brava and, as a young boy, painted many scenes of the Spanish landscape near his home.

As a child, he was surrounded by women—his mother, sisters, aunts, grandmother, and a nurse—who spoiled him. He grew up wild and rebellious but also craved isolation and spent hours by himself.

His childhood was strange and tortured. Dalí's older brother, also named Salvador, died at the age of two from the stomach flu before Dalí was born. The loss of the boy caused his parents to feel grief for years; they kept a portrait of the young child on the wall in their bedroom. As for Dalí, he was haunted by the image of his brother his whole life, believing that his parents conceived him

Gala Dalí was Salvador Dalí's wife, and she also served as his muse for many of his paintings.

Federico García Lorca

Federico García Lorca was a Spanish poet, play-wright, and theatre director. His 1927 play *Mariana Pineda*, based on the life of Spanish liberalist Mariana de Pineda Muñoz, opened in Barcelona, Spain, and was well-received. Salvador Dalí produced the stage settings for the play.

Lorca first met Dalí at the Residencia de Estudiantes in Madrid in 1923 along with filmmaker Luis Buñuel and the famous writer, Pepín Bello. While all four of them were friends,

Federico García Lorca (left) and Salvador Dalí (right) were close friends.

1. Quoted in David Smith, "Were Spain's Two Artistic Legends Secret Gay Lovers?," *Guardian*, October 28, 2007. www.theguardian.com/uk/2007/oct/28/spain.books.
2. Quoted in Smith, "Were Spain's Two Artistic Legends Secret Gay Lovers?"
3. Quoted in Carles Geli, "Dalí and Lorca's Games of Seduction," El País, June 20, 2013. elpais.com/elpais/2013/06/20/inenglish/1371734269_018888.html.

Dalí and Lorca were the closest. Rumors circulated that their relationship went beyond just a friendship. The pair remained close up until Lorca's assassination at the beginning of the Spanish Civil War in 1936.

Years later, it was discovered the two friends had exchanged several letters. Forty letters from Dalí to Lorca were found but only seven from Lorca to Dalí. Two explanations for the loss of letters are Ana María, Dalí's sister, who sold a lot of her brother's things after the Spanish Civil War, or Gala, Dalí's wife, who had access to the letters and may have destroyed many of them out of jealousy.

In 2008, the film *Little Ashes* depicted the relationship between Dalí and Lorca, played by Robert Pattinson and Javier Beltrán, respectively. After extensive research on the two artists' relationship, screenwriter Philippa Goslett claimed, "It's clear something happened, no question ... When you look at the letters it's clear something more was going on there. It began as a friendship, became more intimate."[1] Goslett also described how Dalí felt after Lorca's passing: "[Dalí] was really haunted by Lorca for the rest of his life and talked about him incessantly—more than his wife, Gala."[2] When Dalí was on his deathbed the nurse taking care of him could only understand one thing he said: "My friend Lorca."[3]

as a replacement for the first Salvador. He once said, "All the eccentricities I commit, I do because I wish to prove to myself that I am not the dead brother, but the living one."[21]

Dalí staged the first exhibition of his paintings at the age of 14. Four years later, he enrolled in the Royal Academy of Fine Arts of San Fernando in Madrid, which was Spain's top art school.

He was quickly recognized as the school's top student, but by then, he had started to experiment with abstraction. He was impressed with the Cubist paintings of Picasso, whose style he wanted to imitate. This angered his teachers, who insisted that he concentrate on Impressionism. Dalí, who had long been interested in the meaning of his own dreams, started reading books by Sigmund Freud. He also started supporting Socialist politics.

At the Royal Academy, Dalí fought with his teachers and concluded they were incapable of teaching him. In 1923, the school's administrators found an excuse to expel him. To break up a student protest, the school identified Dalí as a ringleader and kicked him out for a year. Returning home, he was briefly imprisoned for his Socialist activities. Back in Madrid following his suspension, Dalí studied at the Royal Academy for another two years. He continued to experiment with abstract styles and fight with his teachers. Finally, in late 1926 at the age of 22, he was kicked out for good.

Artist Outcast

Dalí maintained a harsh relationship with his teachers at the Royal Academy, but there is no question that he honed his skills as a stylist under their instruction. Indeed, one of Dalí's most important contributions to Surrealism is his work as a stylist: His paintings are very intricate; in his work, the tiniest details are painted with photographic clarity. The influence of Impressionism can be found in his use of bright colors. The Costa Brava landscapes he painted as a boy show up often in the backgrounds of his Surrealist paintings.

Dalí's paintings include many of the fundamental aspects of Surrealist art. For example, he linked objects that would appear to have no association with one another into a single image. Also, Dalí often depicted objects performing functions that they do not normally perform. In the *Metamorphosis of Narcissus*, which Dalí painted in 1937, he depicted a flower growing out of a cracked egg; in his 1938 painting *Apparition of Face and Fruit Dish on a Beach*, a man's head is used as a fruit bowl, and in *The Burning Giraffe* from 1937, he painted a woman's torso and leg as a chest of drawers. These were only some of the images that Dalí displayed in those paintings; each painting included many more images, most intertwined with one another, often providing a challenge to the eye to try to make sense of the action. In *Apparition of Face and Fruit Dish on a Beach*, a close inspection of the painting reveals that not only is the fruit dish turned into the face, but the chin, lips, and nose of the face form the back of a sitting woman. British art historian Paul Moorhouse wrote,

In these works Dalí pushed the phenomenon of images within images further than either he or [Surrealism's] earlier exponents had achieved … In Apparition of Face and Fruit Dish on a Beach *the complexity of the image challenges the observer to decode its matrix of hidden appearances … The bowl of fruit becomes a face, the face becomes a seated woman … Dalí's mastery in simultaneously asserting and denying appearance is reflected in this work.*[22]

The watch faces in *Th[e Persistence] of Memory* challenge the v[iewer to find] a purpose in the images o[f a way of] telling of time. In fact, th[e watches] are not intended to tell tim[e; instead,] they suggest the universe i[s infinite and] has no clock. In the backg[round of the] painting, Dalí has paint[ed the] cliffs of Cadaqués on the

The Persistence of Memory *is Dalí's most recognized work.*

Art critic Robert Goff suggested that Dalí placed the cliffs in the background to show that they would remain standing for thousands of years. "In the Dalían universe, soft objects are detestable: They are powerless and putrefying," Goff wrote. "Only hard objects, such as the rocks of Cadaqués in the background, have worth: Time has no power over them."[23]

Away from the canvas, Dalí craved the attention of the press, which helped shed light on the Surrealist movement. His desire for fame and wealth made him no friends among other Surrealists, who accused him of being more interested in money than in furthering the goals of Surrealist art. In 1934, after Dalí accepted a commission to provide Surrealist paintings to advertise a company that manufactured women's stockings, Breton declared Dalí a traitor to the movement. Breton and the other Surrealists believed their art should not be commercialized. To insult the artist, Breton rearranged the letters in Salvador Dalí's name into the term "avida dollars,"[24] which translates roughly into "eager for dollars." Dalí shot back, "The only difference between me and the Surrealists is that I am a Surrealist."[25] The rift between Dalí and the other Surrealists would never heal; until the ends of their lives, Breton and the others regarded Dalí as an outcast.

Man Ray

While Dalí was born into the European privileged class, Man Ray was raised among far more modest means. Born in 1890 in Philadelphia to Russian Jewish immigrants, Ray's father was a tailor. As a child, Ray was surrounded by needles, flat irons, fabric, mannequins, and spools of thread. In later years, these objects would dominate his artwork. His 1921 Dadaist photograph, *Cadeau* (in English, *Gift*) shows a common flat iron, but with 14 spikes protruding from the surface that would otherwise come into contact with the article of clothing to be ironed.

Ray's artistic talent blossomed while he attended high school in New York, where his family opened a tailor shop when he was seven years old. His talent in his high school mechanical drawing and lettering classes prompted New York University to offer him a scholarship to study architecture, but he turned it down because he desired to be a painter. After high school, he supported himself as a commercial artist and took lessons in fine art when he could afford them.

In 1915, the Daniel Gallery in New York staged an exhibition of his work. He also met Duchamp that year. Duchamp introduced Ray to Dadaism, and soon he was creating art in that style. His 1920 sculpture *New York* depicts a tall bottle filled with steel ball bearings. The piece is similar to Duchamp's "readymades"—ordinary objects that the artist chooses to recognize as art. New York art curator Ingrid Schaffner said Ray's work from this period challenged people to look beyond the physical object he used in the sculpture and appreciate the piece for the idea it means to convey. She wrote, "Using everyday items, often mass-produced, Man Ray created objects, like *New York*, a glass bottle of ball bearings, that

Man Ray started out as a Dadaist and later became a Surrealist.

Lee Miller

At 19 years old, Elizabeth Lee Miller, most commonly referred to as Lee Miller, was almost hit by a car in Manhattan. Luckily, Condé Nast, publisher of *Vogue*, prevented her from being run over. After this incident, Nast helped her launch a modeling career. Antony Penrose, Miller's only son, described his mother's feelings toward modeling: "She loved it at first ... but quickly became bored, seeing it as vacuous [lacking ideas or intelligence] and shallow ... Lee survived because she morphed into becoming a photographer."[1]

After losing interest in the modeling world, she left New York, moved to Paris, and became a photographer. She persuaded Man Ray to teach her photography. After a short time, they began a relationship, and she became his muse.

During this time, she met other artists, such as Pablo Picasso and Max Ernst. She also appeared in Jean Cocteau's film *Le Sang d'un Poète* in 1929. Ray and Miller broke up in 1932. As they went their separate ways, the loss sent Ray into despair. It was during this time that he made some of his most famous works, including *A l'Heure de l'Observatoire—Les Amoureux*. The lips painted in this work are said to be those of Miller.

1. Quoted in Pat Parker, "Lee Miller: The Woman in Hitler's Bathtub," *The Telegraph*, December 2, 2016. www.telegraph.co.uk/photography/what-to-see-lee-miller-woman-hitlers-bathtub/.

captured the tension of working and living bottled up in a landscape of skyscrapers. These objects relate to Duchamp's Readymades by shifting attention from the art object to the *ideas* that transform it into a work of art."[26]

Gallery owners, art critics, and collectors were not yet sold on Dada, and Ray found it difficult to generate interest in his work. In 1921, Ray said, "Dada cannot live in New York. All New York is Dada, and will not tolerate a rival."[27] He left that year for Paris and soon found himself drawn into the Surrealist movement.

Ray's paintings display some familiar Surrealist themes; his 1934 painting *A l'Heure de l'Observatoire—Les Amoureux* (in English, *Observatory Time—The Lovers*) depicts a woman's rouged lips floating across a cloudy sky, while below, a nude reclines alongside a chess board. In later years, he created other versions of this image including a color version with the lips in the sky over just a forest.

Perhaps his most famous painting, which he created in 1938, is *Portrait of the Marquis de Sade*. Ray's study of the famous French nobleman features the marquis constructed of bricks, watching as a mob attacks and sets fire to the Bastille, France's notorious prison. French art historian Marina Vanci-Perahim said the painting and others are significant additions to Surrealist art because they add a three-dimensional perspective to the genre. For example, she wrote, in *Portrait of the Marquis de Sade*, Ray painted the brickwork curving around the face: "No longer reducing his images to two dimensions, he developed an illusionist pictorial space that was better adapted to his dreamscapes."[28]

Man Ray's Photography Techniques

Ray was an important surrealist painter, but it is as a photographer that the artist expanded Surrealism into other genres of creativity. *Le Violon d'Ingres* (in English, *The Violin of Ingres*) is one of Ray's most famous photographs. Produced in 1924, it depicts images of F holes—the curvy sound holes found on the face of a stringed instrument—inked onto the naked back of a woman.

Ray also used the solarization process in Surrealist photography. The technique is produced in the darkroom by giving prints under development a second exposure to light. If done properly, the technique results in a fuzzy black halo around the object in the photo, giving the image a dreamy quality that helps add to the surreal feeling of the photograph.

Another Surrealist style Ray brought to photography could be found in his "Rayographs." These were photographs made by placing ordinary household objects onto photographic paper, then exposing them to light. After the prints were developed, they depicted eerie silhouettes of the objects. Among his Rayograph images are depictions of keys, wire coils, human profiles, and sewing needles. According to Schaffner, Ray's skill at solarization as well as his development of the Rayograph show that the artist found a way to merge the real with the unreal. Schaffner wrote, "Surrealist photography exploited our basic assumption that photography presented reality as we 'saw' it and then shocked us by going beyond that reality, or by undermining it."[29]

René Magritte

While Dalí was flamboyant and Ray was a willing dweller of the Parisian café community, Magritte was quiet and reserved and preferred to have supper at home with his family. As Dalí sought wealth and fame, Magritte preferred to live the life more familiar to middle-class working people. He painted in his own home, setting up his easel in his dining room.

His 1953 painting *Golconde* (in English, *Golconda*, which is the name of a former fortress city in India) is a self-portrait. The painting shows Magritte in numerous duplications of himself, dressed in suit and bowler hat, raining down on a cityscape. British art historian David Sylvester said that in *Golconde*, Magritte makes a statement about the inability of individuals to

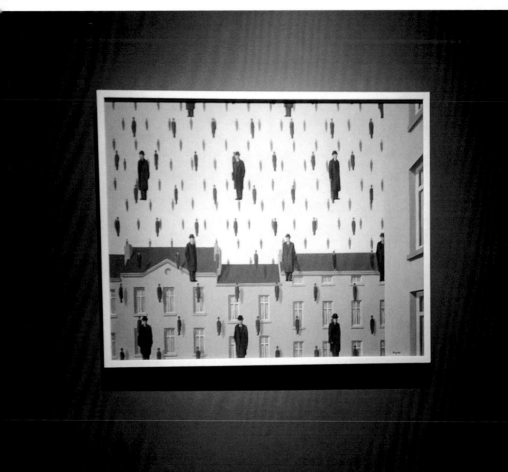

Surrealist painter René Magritte made a statement about individuals in a cluttered society in his 1953 painting Golconde.

assert themselves in a cluttered society. "They seem stuck there in space like repetitions of an ornamental device," Sylvester wrote of the many replications of Magritte in the painting. "In fact they are parts of a pattern like a wallpaper pattern, infinitely repeatable and extendable. They seem a sample of an infinity of identically helpless beings."[30]

Magritte's paintings also show the whimsical side of Surrealism. His

1937 painting *La Reproduction Interdite* (in English, *Not to be Reproduced*) depicts his model looking into a mirror to see the back of his own head—the same image the viewer sees as they examine the painting. His 1934 painting *Collective Invention* depicts a fish crawling out of the ocean, its tail fins replaced by a woman's legs. It is the opposite of the classic image of the mermaid. It is a humorous image, but some critics have suggested it shows that Magritte did have a darker side. His mother, Regina Magritte, committed suicide by drowning herself in the Sambre River. "In *Collective Invention,* which turns a woman into a fish from the waist up, he alludes to his mother's drowned body," Bradley Collins Jr. wrote, "and [he] mocks her—by jumping into the river she has become no better than a fish."[31]

Max Ernst

Like many of the other Surrealists, such as Ray, Ernst made the transition from Dadaism to Surrealism. His 1920 Dada painting *The Master's Bedroom, It's Worth Spending a Night There* shows various animals—a snake, miniature whale, bat, fish, bear, and lamb—occupying a bedroom, although their human owner is not in the picture. The lack of the human prompts the viewer to wonder whether it truly is worth spending the night. Spanish art historian José María Faerna said the artist's use of perspective in the painting, which depicts wide spaces between the furniture and the animals, makes it even less inviting to the visitor. "The sense of unreality is ominously heightened by the extreme rendering of perspective and by the precarious placement of the furniture,"[32] he wrote.

By 1921, Ernst left Dadaism to concentrate on Surrealism. That was the year he painted *The Elephant Celebes.* Like Ray, Ernst looked for new ways to use the tools and materials of the artist. He helped develop a technique known as frottage, which involves making rubbings of textured surfaces, which are then transferred to the canvas.

Ernst discovered the frottage method one evening when he stopped at a hotel at Pornic on the French Atlantic coast and noticed the rough, textured surface of the floorboards. Ernst dropped sheets of paper onto the floor, dropped to his knees, and rubbed the surface with a pencil. He was awestruck by the patterns

After Max Ernst transitioned from Dadaism to Surrealism, he created his work The Elephant Celebes.

from the rubbings and
ed them into his work.
fected the technique
comania, which added
tical atmosphere to his
calcomania involves
a sheet of paper or
sometimes glass, then pressing the
painted surface onto a canvas. Ernst
believed that transferring the paintings
in this way helped make them more
abstract and gave him a better insight
into the images he believed were alive
in his subconscious. His painting *Day*

and Night, which he completed in 1942, was produced through the decalcomania process and shows a number of intricately painted pylons rising from what appears to be a prehistoric landscape. Various parts of the painting display bright colors, signifying day, while others are painted in dim shades, signifying night.

Day and Night was painted as war raged in Europe. Ernst had been displaced by the war — he had been imprisoned for a time by the Nazis, then released. Forced to sneak out of Europe, Ernst made his way to America and painted *Day and Night* shortly after arriving. Art historian John Russell suggested that *Day and Night* depicts Ernst's attempt to remain in control of his life and art, regardless of what was happening in Europe. "His determination to get these opposites and antitheses into one and the same picture may have resulted, I think, from a determination to not be overwhelmed by the paradoxes and contradictions of wartime life," Russell wrote. "Somehow, the artist had to be the master of them: his ability to order experience must rise above whatever was put in its way."[33]

Joan Miró

Dalí's mentor, Joan Miró, was one of the founders of the Surrealist movement, but he resisted that description for his work, believing himself free to work in a number of styles. Still, Miró sought to probe his subconscious in search of Surrealist images. To find these images Miró attempted to induce a hallucinogenic state by starving himself and depriving himself of sleep. His most famous work, *Harlequin's Carnival*, was conceived while Miró was under the influence of sleep deprivation. The painting, which Miró produced between 1924 and 1925, includes dozens of images such as streamers blowing in the wind, masks, cats, guitars, mustaches, fish, winged creatures, and other shapes that Miró believed he had drawn from his subconscious mind. French art historian Jacques Lassaigne said *Harlequin's Carnival* is populated by many diverse images but nevertheless is held together by a number of visual techniques

Miró deprived himself of food and sleep, which he believed helped him tap into his subconcious mind.

Miró employed in the painting. He wrote,

Extremely complex but never over-loaded, the composition is built up quite straightforwardly around the central figure, a man playing a gui-tar. The wire-drawn axis of his body, duplicated by a white spiral, bisects the canvas vertically, and is divided

horizontally by the line formed by the junction of the floor and wall, and also by an arm ending in a monstrous hand. This intersection, though twice repeated, is not pronounced enough to disturb the overall balance, but acts on the contrary as a unifying factor.[34]

In the painting, the figure of Harlequin — a clown who first appeared in 15th-century Italian comic theater — can be found in the upper left-hand corner of the painting. Lassaigne suggested that Miró painted Harlequin as a self-portrait. "He represents … Miró himself," Lassaigne wrote, "watcher and donor of this strange masterwork."[35]

André Masson

Another artist who experimented with sleep deprivation was Masson, who brought a Cubist influence to Surrealism and mostly used automatism in creating his work. He also denied himself food, hoping to enter a trance so that he could explore his subconscious. Like other Surrealists, he experimented with techniques and materials — he often coated his canvases with glue and then threw sand onto them, painting on top of the shapes that were formed. Masson believed the artist should not be able to control the surface on which they painted — that was why the sand was tossed on at random.

One of his most famous "sand pictures" is titled *Battle of Fishes*, which he completed in 1927. Painted through automatism while Masson was in a sleep-deprived trance, the picture shows various line drawings of fish attacking one another. The most noticeable use of color in the painting is seen through blobs of red paint — symbolizing blood — while the sand has taken on the look of a mountain, suggesting that the fish were not necessarily fighting underwater and, perhaps, the fish were not really fish. Masson, a French army soldier gravely wounded in World War I, often used the canvas to make statements about war. Schneede wrote,

In the sand pictures, Masson tried to break free from the restrictions and rules of painting. What has been gained is a kind of breakthrough, an art that transcends the boundaries of the conventional

Masson believed the artist should not have control over the surface they paint on.

picture. The thematic content of Battle of Fish and similar works is the trauma of war translated into the animal world … War and death are important themes in Masson's work.[36]

By the late 1920s, Masson found the Surrealist movement too confining and started working in far more abstract genres. In the years to come, the work of Masson as well as the other Surrealists would provide the foundations for many other artists. The Surrealists' work, practices, and views would also serve as inspiration for the development of future art movements, such as Abstract Expressionism and Pop Art. Both art movements display subtle, or sometimes extremely evident, signs of being influenced by Surrealism, just as all future art movements will undoubtedly include hints of these varied characteristics as well.

Artists Influenced by Surrealists

As time went on, new art movements stole the spotlight from Surrealism, creating new spectacles, which caught the attention of the general public. All of a sudden, people were less interested in what the Surrealists were doing and more focused on these artists who were inspired by them and were becoming the next generation of trendsetters in the art world.

The major art movement directly following the Surrealism movement was Abstract Expressionism. Abstract Expressionists who dominated the art world in the 1940s and 1950s included Jackson Pollock and Willem de Kooning. Later, the Pop Art created by Andy Warhol in the 1960s and 1970s employed some of the techniques first explored by the Surrealists. Meanwhile,

artists working in America and elsewhere, including Dorothea Tanning in the United States and Frida Kahlo in Mexico, explored their own Surrealist images and have become recognized as important Surrealist artists.

Starting in the late 1930s, Dalí, Ernst, and many of the other founding members of the Surrealist movement fled Europe to escape the clouds of war that hovered over the continent. Many of them settled in America, where they created Surrealist art and gave exhibitions of their work but, with the exception of Dalí, preferred to live quietly and out of the spotlight. Still, other artists observed their work and found themselves drawn to the genre and anxious to adapt the techniques of Surrealism to their own art. Schneede wrote, "Now that Surrealism was beginning to pass into the hands of a new generation, there were new principles, new goals."[37]

Picasso Avoids Joining Surrealists

The Surrealists had been influencing other artists long before they crossed the Atlantic Ocean. Among the most renowned European artists who dabbled in Surrealism was Picasso, who had been friendly with Breton and Miró and admired the work of Dalí.

Breton, whose portrait was painted a half-dozen times by Picasso, tried to lure Picasso into Surrealism. He believed that Picasso's painting *Man*

While some say Pablo Picasso helped lay the foundation for Surrealist art, he never truly joined the Surrealist movement.

with a Clarinet, which was created between 1911 and 1912, was the first truly Surrealist painting. The work, which was created in the Cubist style, features mostly muted gray and brown tones. The clarinet player is displayed mostly through the use of triangular shapes. Breton suggested that Man with a Clarinet laid the foundation for all future Surrealist art.

Still, Picasso never formally joined the Surrealist school, preferring to paint and interpret what he saw with his own eyes rather than explore the depths of his subconscious for inspiration. However, Picasso was fascinated with expressing the dark side of human thought—a fascination he shared with all the Surrealists. For example, one of Picasso's paintings, Head of a Woman, features an abstract rendering of a woman's face; the Surrealist influence can be seen in how Picasso painted the teeth—as though they are daggers.

New Art Movements Reach the United States

Even though he remained on the outer edge of Surrealist art, an artist of Picasso's stature nevertheless added authenticity to a movement that was greeted with skepticism outside France. Certainly, Picasso's reputation helped sell Surrealism in the United States, where the movement found an audience among young art students who were starting to form their own ideas that would pave the way for Abstract Expressionism.

Many American artists had their first exposure to Surrealist and Dadaist art at a 1936 exhibition at the MoMA in New York. TIME magazine, which covered the exhibition, said,

Inside the front door of Manhattan's Museum of Modern Art this week, oblong slabs of glass painted with black stripes revolved steadily under a six foot pair of red lips painted by Artist Man Ray. In other galleries throughout the building were a black felt head with a necklace of cinema film and zippers for eyes; a stuffed parrot on a hollow log containing a doll's leg; a teacup, plate and spoon covered entirely with fur.[38]

Jackson Pollock

One of the artists who studied those images was Jackson Pollock, a founder of Abstract Expressionism. Pollock was fascinated by automatism and determined to use that technique to produce a new school of images.

Abstract Expressionists paint wild, bizarre, and colorful scenes that appear to have no logical form. Many do not use normal painting techniques. One of the traits of Surrealism that attracted the Abstract Expressionists was the way the Surrealists often began their paintings or drawings. In many cases, a Surrealist would pick a place on the canvas at random and make a

Guggenheim Beginnings

The woman most responsible for introducing Surrealism to the American art community was Marguerite "Peggy" Guggenheim, a New York socialite and member of the wealthy Guggenheim family. Born in 1898, Guggenheim moved to Paris as a young woman, and she joined the circle of artists who lived in the French capital following World War I. She became friendly with Duchamp and Ray, for whom she modeled.

With her inheritance she acquired an impressive collection of Surrealist art, which included works by Dalí, Miró, Magritte, and Ernst, to whom she was married from 1941 to 1946. During World War II, Guggenheim opened an art gallery in New York City that specialized in Dadaism and Surrealism but also featured the works of Jackson Pollock and other American abstract artists. She named the gallery Art of This Century.

In 1943, Guggenheim hosted the first of two exhibitions with all female artists titled *Exhibition by 31 Women*, which included Leonora Carrington, Leonor Fini, Valentine Hugo, Djuna Barnes, Kay Sage, Dorothea Tanning, and Frida Kahlo. All the artists were under 30, except Barnes, and the group represented 16 different nationalities. The second exhibition, *The Women*, included works by Louise Bourgeois, Lee Krasner, and more.

pencil mark or smudge or a streak with a paintbrush, and then, through the process of automatism, they let the rest of the artwork fall into place. The randomness of Surrealist art fascinated the Abstract Expressionists, and they were eager to begin their paintings in a similar fashion.

Pollock studied Surrealism and admired the work of Masson, who experimented with a technique in which he would simply let the paint from his brush drip onto the canvas. The artist adopted the drip method and regarded it as a form of automatism. His friend and fellow Abstract Expressionist, Peter Busa, recalled watching him work. Busa said, "He talked about the free-agent, the element in Surrealism where you don't touch the canvas, where you let the paint fall."[39]

Still, Pollock and the other American Abstract Expressionists were not prone to become Surrealists themselves. Most of the European Surrealists did not speak English. With the exception of Dalí, the Surrealists rarely lectured, gave interviews, or accepted students. May Rosenberg, the wife of influential art critic Harold Rosenberg, wrote, "The Surrealists arrived like visiting royalty, bearers of sacred visions to the heathens; trippers among

Even though Jackson Pollock was an Abstract Expressionist, the influence of Surrealism could be seen in his work.

the lollipops."[40]

Pollock looked beyond the insensitivities and the quirkiness of the European Surrealists, concentrating mostly on their techniques. As he became an established member of the American abstract art community, Pollock attempted to probe his subconscious thoughts for inspiration. His 1943 painting *The She-Wolf* shows just how much his work was influenced by Surrealism. The painting depicts an image of a bull standing against a background of broad streaks of black and curls of color. Art critics studied the image intently and were unable to find the image of a wolf in the painting—largely because Pollock had not painted one. Pollock's friend, the artist James Brooks, said that the image clearly formed itself in the deepest part of Pollock's subconscious mind: "[Jackson's] unconscious came through. In a sense, he walked right into another world."[41]

Tanning and Hare

Despite the reluctance of the Abstract Expressionists to fully adopt Surrealism, there were some American artists who embraced the genre. When he arrived in America, Max Ernst met Dorothea Tanning, a New York-based artist. The two would eventually marry. When they met in 1942, Tanning was working on a painting of a seminude woman—a self-portrait of herself

at 30—opening a door to reveal a series of other doors opening as well. This painting, titled *Birthday*, featured a winged lemur crouched at her feet. Around the woman's waist, Tanning painted a skirt of roots; around the woman's shoulders, she painted a puffy-sleeved purple and gold jacket with frilly cuffs, as though the woman has just stepped out of Europe's Renaissance era. Schneede wrote,

If we wanted to assume that the picture has symbolic significance, we might take it for a self-portrait in which the skirt of many roots points to a closeness to nature while the Renaissance jacket may suggest an affinity with art and with the many Renaissance pictures of Venus. In such a context, the open doors could be interpreted as leading to various new beginnings in the artist's life.[42]

Ernst declared that he intended to marry the artist and keep the painting. "I want to spend the rest of my life with Dorothea," he said. "This picture is part of that life."[43]

Another American accepted into the Surrealist movement was David Hare, a painter, sculptor, and photographer. Like Ray, Hare experimented with the photographer's tools and processes. He found that he could give his negatives an eerie

Dorothea Tanning and Max Ernst married in 1946.

effect by heating them during the development process, which caused the negatives to ripple and distort. He called the automatist process "heat-age." Although Hare experimented with Surrealist photography, his sculptures are regarded as his most Surrealist work. He created complex bronze, steel, and rock sculptures. Hare's sculpture *Sunrise*, which he completed in 1955, features a sun-like figure held aloft over a rocky Earth by metal rods. He also included drops of rain, two moons, and a star. In the 1960s, the Albright Knox Art Gallery in Buffalo, New York, wrote to Hare and requested a statement on *Sunrise*. According to the Albright Knox,

> *The answer to the question "Why would you sculpt a sunrise?" came a good deal easier to David Hare than that to "How do you sculpt a sunrise?" The artist wrote that he embarked [upon]* Sunrise *and other such landscape sculptures primarily as artistic challenges or dares. In each case, the main point "was first to make a sculpture from a subject which seemed highly unlikely as a sculptural material, the interest in this being the difficulty of the problem and also its newness."*[44]

When Breton arrived in America, he collaborated with Hare on the journal *VVV*, which promoted and analyzed Surrealist art in the United States.

Andy Warhol

By the 1960s, Pop Art had become a major force in the American art world. Its most legendary pioneer was Andy Warhol, whose work includes portraits of Campbell soup cans and oversized replicas of Brillo soap pad boxes. He was also known for colorful portraits of celebrities such as Marilyn Monroe and Elvis Presley. He decorated his New York studio, which he called the "Factory," completely in silver, covering every square inch with silver paint or with aluminum foil. This bizarre display of modern art was embraced by art critics who believed Warhol represented the first wave of a new generation of hip artists. To show off the newly decorated studio, Warhol threw a party and invited the press. The reporters and partygoers who saw the Factory decked out in silver must surely have felt the presence of the Surrealists in the room with them. One news reporter wrote,

> *The whole place is Reynolds wrap, the ceiling, the pipes, the walls. The floor has been painted silver. All the cabinets have been painted silver. The odd assortment of stools and chairs are silver. And the bathroom is silver lined and painted, including the toilet bowl and flushing mechanism.*[45]

Andy Warhol was known for his replicas of Brillo soap pad boxes.

Warhol may not have fully embraced Surrealism, but wrapping an ordinary room floor to ceiling in aluminum foil certainly merged the real world with the unreal. In fact, Warhol had experimented with Surrealist techniques for years. During the 1950s, he perfected a technique known as the "blotted line." He used pen and ink to draw an image, then blotted a clean sheet of paper over the wet ink to create a runny and abstract form. The blotted line technique helped Warhol define his modern style; nevertheless, it was a technique closely related to decalcomania, which was perfected by Ernst some 30 years earlier.

Warhol's portraits of Campbell soup cans seemed a lot like updated versions of Duchamp's readymades, which led experts to contemplate the difference between Dada and Pop Art. Bruce H. Hinrichs, a professor of psychology who has studied modern art, wrote, "Andy Warhol and other Pop artists painted ... images of soup cans and similarly mundane, ordinary objects, forcing the viewer to look again and carefully at objects of common perception. The ironic upshot ... was that the Surrealist object was praised for its strangeness and the Pop Art object for its unstrangeness!"[46]

Dalí and Warhol

During the 1970s, Dalí and his wife Gala visited New York frequently. They welcomed Warhol into their circle. Now in his 70s, Dalí had lost none of the flamboyance that catapulted him to fame some 40 years before. He carried a gold scepter, gave lavish parties, and enjoyed dining with celebrities in New York's bistros. He always invited the attention of photographers and hoped to see his name in the tabloid newspapers.

By now, Warhol had been making his celebrity portraits by taking photographs of his subjects before blowing them up into very large prints. Next, he traced the images on canvas. Then, he used the blotted line technique to give them an abstract feel. Finally, Warhol colored them—often

Roy Lichtenstein

Another American artist who was influenced by Surrealists and Abstract Expressionists was Roy Lichtenstein. He is grouped with the likes of Warhol, James Rosenquist, and Claes Oldenburg; all of them are known for originating the Pop Art Movement, which began in the mid-to-late 1950s. His first paintings were inspired by imagery from popular comic strips and advertisements. Some of the cartoons he chose to draw were recognizable characters, such as Mickey Mouse, Donald Duck, and Popeye. As his art career progressed, he began to paint more generic human figures that represented comic book characters of that period. Another pattern he became known for borrowing and using in his artwork was Benday dots:

> Most famously, Lichtenstein appropriated the Benday dots, the minute mechanical patterning used in commercial engraving, to convey texture and gradations of color—a stylistic language synonymous with his subject matter. The dots became a trademark device forever identified with Lichtenstein and Pop Art.[1]

Lichtenstein's most famous paintings are 1963's *Drowning Girl,* in which a girl is seen crying immersed in waves, and 1964's *Oh Jeff...I Love You, Too...But...*, which depicts a blonde-haired woman on the phone. In both images, Lichtenstein utilized Benday dots, which made it seem as if he was "painting digital pixels before there were pixels."[2]

Some critics of Lichtenstein's art claimed it was not original art, but merely copying cultural imagery. Additionally, the comic artists he copied suffered, receiving no payment or credit for the work Lichtenstein copied while Lichtenstein made millions. In 1964, *Life* magazine published an article about Lichtenstein with the headline "Is He the Worst Artist in the U.S.?" Lichtenstein explained how his art was different from the comic strips he used as reference for his works:

> I think my work is different from comic strips—but I wouldn't call it transformation; I don't think that whatever is meant by it is important to art ... And my work is actually different from comic strips in that every mark is really in a different place, however slight the difference seems to some ... People also consider my work to be anti-art in the same way they consider it pure depiction, "not transformed". I don't feel it is anti-art.[3]

1. Avis Berman, "Biography," Roy Lichtenstein Foundation, accessed on June 11, 2018. lichtensteinfoundation.org/biography/.
2. Quoted in Susan Stamberg, "One Dot at a Time, Lichtenstein Made Art Pop," NPR, October 15, 2012. www.npr.org/2012/10/15/162807890/one-dot-at-a-time-lichtenstein-made-art-pop.
3. Quoted in Artspace Editors, "In This 1963 Interview, Roy Lichtenstein 'Doubts' Pop Art Will Have a Lasting Influence," Artspace, September 22, 2017. www.artspace.com/magazine/interviews_ features/book_report/roy-lichtenstein-what-is-pop-art-55006.

Roy Lichtenstein was famous for his use of Benday (also called Ben-Day) dots.

with fluorescent tones. Although the portraits are not regarded as Surrealist works, Warhol's technique gave them a Surrealist look. Dalí admired them greatly, but when Warhol offered to photograph Gala Dalí for one of the portraits, the artist flatly refused. "The strength of Gala ... is in her privacy," he insisted. "Gala never is photo-graphed!"[47] To make Warhol feel better, though, Dalí did acknowledge that he had risen to second place on the list of Dalí's favorite artists. First place was, of course, still held by Dalí himself.

There is no question that Warhol was influenced by the techniques of Surrealism, but he was never one to explore the depths of his subconscious thought—he was much more comfortable gossiping with celebrities at New York City discos. However, he was the type of artist who delighted in shocking the public, and for that he owed a great debt to the Surrealists.

Frida Kahlo

The Surrealists' influence was not confined to U.S. artists such as Pollock, Tanning, and Warhol; Surrealists were also influencing artists such as Frida Kahlo in Mexico. Kahlo had suffered through many personal tragedies, such as having her right leg deformed by polio and witnessing the bloodshed of the Mexican Revolution as a young girl. As a medical student, she was severely injured in a bus

Frida Kahlo is shown here standing beside her 1939 painting The Two Fridas.

accident that would force her to drop out of medical school and live in pain for the rest of her life. She underwent 30 operations in her lifetime. The accident also damaged her reproductive organs, making it impossible for her to have children.

She used art to reveal her psychological distress. Kahlo produced 143 paintings in her lifetime, 55 of which were self-portraits. Her 1946 self-portrait *The Wounded Deer* is a typical example of Kahlo's Surrealism. The painting depicts Kahlo's head on the body of a deer that has been pierced by arrows. Art historian Hayden Herrera said the painting tells a lot about Kahlo's tortured life:

In [the painting] Frida presents herself with the body of a young stag and her own head crowned with antlers. Like Frida, the deer is prey to suffering. Pierced by nine arrows, he stares out at the viewer from a forest enclosure …

The deer's youthful vigor contrasts with the decay of old tree trunks, whose broken branches and knots correspond to his wounds. Beneath him a slender branch broken from a young tree alludes to Frida's and the deer's broken youth and imminent death …

In Aztec belief the deer was the sign for the right foot; even with

Frida's various operations, the condition of her right foot continued to worsen, and the deer could have been a kind of talisman. The arrows in the deer may, like the arrows in valentine hearts, point to pain in love.[48]

Kahlo met Breton in 1938 during a visit by the Surrealist poet to Mexico. He was impressed with her work and used his contacts to arrange for an exhibition of her art in New York. Kahlo was one of several Mexican artists who experimented with Surrealism. Others included Kahlo's husband, Diego Rivera, who also painted in the Cubist style; José Clemente Orozco, whose large murals often featured Surrealist images; and David Alfaro Siqueiros, who used colors as brightly and boldly as Dalí.

The Mind of Leonora Carrington

Another Mexican Surrealist was Leonora Carrington. British-born, she met Ernst in France and worked closely with him. When the Germans invaded France, Carrington fled to Madrid, Spain, where she suffered a mental breakdown in 1940. When her parents became involved in her medical care, she was institutionalized and confined to an asylum in Santander, Spain. There she was given powerful antipsychotic drugs and treated with a drug that mimicked the convulsions of electro-convulsive therapy, which is when small electric currents are passed through the brain. In 1941, she escaped the psychiatric treatments by marrying Mexican diplomat Renato Leduc, who helped her secure passage to New York City. In 1942, she left New York for Mexico and became a Mexican citizen, while also divorcing Leduc.

In Mexico, she painted in the Surrealist style. Typical of her Surrealist work is the 1945 painting *The Pleasures of Dagobert*, which features dozens of surreal images — fire, volcanoes, forests, a winding staircase, a woman adrift in a small boat, a beast rising from a pool of water, a ghostly apparition streaking overhead, and a bearded king led on horseback by a child, among others. According to British art historian Dawn Adès, Carrington's talent for Surrealism blossomed in Mexico, where she found a country entering modern civilization while slowly shaking off the mystical beliefs and practices of its people. Carrington enjoyed wading into the street markets of old Mexican cities, where she listened to the tall tales told by the vendors. Carrington was fascinated by the "magic" potions sold by street vendors, and she also believed in alchemy. Clearly, Adès said, Carrington drew inspiration for *The Pleasures of Dagobert* from her forays into Mexican mysticism:

> *Carrington portrays here, with the luminous clarity of her egg tempera technique, complete imaginary worlds ... The different landscapes correspond to the four elements of alchemy and medieval natural history: earth, air, fire and water. There is a definite rhythm to their placings ... Transformations, of the elements, of human, animal, plant, of animate and inanimate, occur at every point.*[49]

Carrington said that many of these images came to her while she fought through the difficulties of mental illness. She said, "I was ... the Moon, the Holy Ghost, a gypsy, an acrobat, Leonora Carrington, and a woman."[50] However, it was Kahlo who Breton declared had most sincerely captured the passion of Surrealism in Mexico. He described Kahlo's art as "a ribbon around a bomb."[51]

Surrealism remained a prominent fixture in the art world and remained influential despite the welcoming of new art movements. All groundbreaking artistic discoveries after the inception of Surrealism in some way paid tribute to the greats who came before them. In the years to come, Surrealists would take their art a step further, challenging social norms and the state of society.

CHAPTER FOUR

Art Advocating Social Change

One aspect that came with the principle ideas of the Surrealism movement was social change. While the art served as an aesthetic, or beautiful, work, its other purpose, at times, was to convey certain messages to its spectators.

Breton and the other early Surrealists were drawn to left-wing politics and supported the Socialists, Communists, and anarchists who attempted to gain prominence in post–World War I Europe. The Surrealists believed the war was caused by a small number of wealthy industrialists and others who sought to profit from the bloodshed of others. Breton and the other Surrealists believed that the common people—the workers—should rise up against the power of the industrialists. He said,

If this were religion, the fervor of our intentions alone would have been enough. The Surrealists in particular gave much of themselves. They had adhered to the view that what was still—and by far—most shocking about the world around them was the subservience in which a miniscule part of the human race held the rest, without any justification whatsoever. Of all the evils this was the most intolerable, since it was entirely within man's power to remedy.[52]

While many of the Surrealist artists followed Breton into Socialism, unlike Breton, few of them sought to become influential in the international Socialist movement. Instead, most of the Surrealists preferred using their art to make political statements. As the Surrealists fled Europe during World War II, many would use their paintings to denounce, or criticize, war. Following the war, Surrealism continued to carry a political message, often in support of public uprisings against corrupt or repressive regimes. For decades, many political movements have looked toward Surrealism for inspiration.

Socialism Activist

Breton was more than just an intellectual Socialist. He wrote about Socialism, addressed assemblies, and traveled extensively, actively promoting the Socialist cause. In 1938, he visited exiled Soviet Communist leader Leon Trotsky in Mexico, where he had been befriended by Kahlo and Rivera. Trotsky, Breton, and Rivera drew up a manifesto, *Towards a Free Revolutionary Art*, which called for artists and writers to use their skills in support of Socialism. The manifesto stated, "The communist revolution is not afraid of art. It realizes that the role of the artist in a decadent capitalist society is determined by the conflict between the individual and various social forms that are hostile to him. This fact alone, insofar as he is conscious of it, makes the artist the natural ally of revolution."[53]

Later, in a Socialist magazine that Breton edited, which was titled *Clé* (in English, *Key*), he wrote that art should be the universal voice of the Socialist movement. "Art has no country, just as the workers have none,"[54] Breton insisted.

Many of the Surrealist artists were not as active politically as Breton; instead, they chose to speak through their canvases. Most of the early Surrealist artists dabbled in the ideology espoused by the German writer Karl Marx, whose 1848 book *The Communist Manifesto* inspired the leaders of the Bolshevik revolution in Russia and led to the establishment of the Soviet Union. The Surrealists were interested in what Marx had to say and not just because they felt workers had been abused by factory owners. Marx also advocated a breakdown of many of the principles of cultured society, such as the abolition of marriage.

Marx's political goals—the establishment of a workers' utopia—struck a chord with the Surrealists. Ray's credentials as a Socialist dated back to his early days in New York before he left for Paris to join the Surrealist movement. He was acquainted with Socialist agitator Emma Goldman and designed some covers for her magazine, *Mother Earth.*

One of the most prominent artists of the era to adopt Communist sympathies was George Grosz, who is regarded as a Dadaist but whose work often contains strong Surrealist images. His most famous painting, *Republican Automatons*, which he painted in 1920, shows two gentlemen standing on a street in Berlin, Germany. One of the

George Grosz's 1921 work Grey Day was his own personal commentary on the inequality within the Weimar Republic.

men has no face; instead, the number 12 is printed across his blank head. The other man in the picture has no top to his head; words and numerals pour out of the opening. Grosz envisioned his fellow Germans as robots following the commands of the Weimar government without question. In the painting, one of the robots holds aloft the German flag. Grosz is given credit for steering Dada toward promoting political messages—a trend that would be embraced by the Surrealists. Art historians H. H. Arnason, Marla F. Prather, and Daniel Wheeler wrote, "Empty-headed, blank-faced, and mutilated automatons parade loyally through the streets of a mechanistic metropolis on their way to vote as they are told. In such works as this, Grosz comes closest to the spirit of the Dadaists and Surrealists."[55]

Surrealists Influenced by Spanish Conflict

Like Grosz, many Surrealists found inspiration in World War I and its aftermath. Another conflict would soon brew on the European continent, touching the lives of some Surrealists and influencing their work and their private lives. The Spanish Civil War lasted from 1936 until 1939 and resulted in a victory for the Fascists under General Francisco Franco, who would go on to lead Spain until his death in 1975. Among the opponents who fought against Franco were Socialists. The dictator treated his opponents harshly, lining up captured prisoners in front of firing squads in his campaign to wipe out Socialism in Spain.

Many of the Surrealists sided with the Socialists. Masson's 1937 painting *Hora de Todos* (in English, *Hour of All*) features grays and blacks and displays many tortured faces. The artist intended the painting as a statement against the bloodshed of the Spanish conflict. In 1946, Magritte contributed *Le Drapeau Noir* (in English, *The Black Flag*), which shows bizarre flying machines hovering in a dark sky over a barren landscape. During the civil war, Franco enlisted the German army to bomb enemy positions in the town of Guernica, which resulted in the deaths of an estimated 1,600 Spaniards, although some historians think around 200 were killed and hundreds more wounded. Magritte produced the painting in response to the massacre. "The first, and also the last, impression the painting makes on us is one of a threat hanging over the world," Hammacher

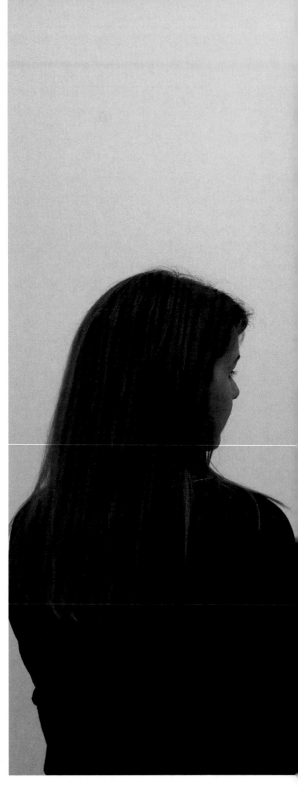

Dalí's Soft Construction with Boiled Beans—Premonition of Civil War *was his own commentary on the Spanish Civil War.*

wrote. "The color is somber, hard, and menacing, and the draftsmanship of the construction is as simple as it is relentlessly accurate."[56]

Dalí also made his own statements against war. In the early 1930s, Dalí and his wife Gala left Paris for a lecture in Barcelona. It was there that Dalí first sensed the country was heading toward revolution because the country was in turmoil with workers on strike and anarchists demonstrating in the streets. Dalí was unable to give the lecture—conditions were deemed unsafe, so instead the Dalís returned to Paris. Shaken by the experience, Dalí showed his fear for the future of his country in his paintings. In 1936, he produced *Soft Construction with Boiled Beans—Premonition of Civil War*. The image shows a tortured figure standing over a desolate landscape. Grappling and clawing beneath the figure are twisted, emaciated arms and legs. Meanwhile, all that is left of value in the countryside is a handful of scattered beans. The painting represents Dalí's vision for the future of Spain after the war. He said,

I painted a geological landscape that had been uselessly revolutionized for thousands of years congealed in its "normal course." The soft structure of that great mass of flesh in civil war I embellished with a few boiled beans, for one could not imagine swallowing all that unconscious meat without the presence (however uninspiring) of some mealy and melancholy vegetable.[57]

Spanish poet Federico García Lorca, who had been instrumental in promoting antifascism among many Spaniards, undoubtedly influenced Dalí's feelings about the coming war. Dalí met Lorca in 1923, when both men resided in a students' residence hall in Madrid. As a student in Madrid, Dalí supported anarchy and radical politics, although these positions would soften in later years. Lorca did not soften his antifascist positions; eventually, he would be murdered by agents acting under Franco's orders.

Miró, also a Spaniard, opposed Franco as well. In 1937, he produced a poster for Franco's opponents that was employed by the movement's leaders to rally opposition to the Fascists. The poster shows an opponent of Fascism with a raised fist and the caption, "In the current struggle I see the antiquated forces of Fascism on one side, and on the other, those of the people, whose immense creative resources will give Spain a drive that will amaze the world."[58]

America Prevails After World War II

Miró and Dalí remained in France during the Spanish Civil War. As Fascism grew in Germany, the Surrealists used their paintings to warn of the coming Nazi threat. Dalí's 1938 painting *Mountain Lake* shows the gigantic handset of a telephone perched in front of a lake. According to Dalí, the telephone represents the fruitless conversations between British Prime Minister Neville Chamberlain and Adolf Hitler that resulted in the Munich Pact, which delivered Czechoslovakia to Nazi hands and set the stage for World War II. To punctuate this point, Dalí drew two snails crawling over the telephone—symbols that peace negotiations were moving too slowly. Another significant image in the painting is the skeleton of a wooden sailing ship. Moorhouse explained the hidden meanings within the painting:

> There is a pervading sense of melancholy and decay … The receiver hangs from a crutch, its cord draped limply from a second, similar support, suggesting that the lines of communication are dead. Snails crawl over the telephone, symbolizing the protracted and hopeless nature of the negotiations. On the horizon the wreck of a boat, the spars of its hull exposed like a ribcage, evokes the end of a voyage.[59]

Of course, the devastation of World War II would not touch Dalí personally. He waited out the war years in the United States in comfort, enjoying the attention of his wealthy American admirers. Dalí fully embraced his new home and thoroughly loved the American people as well as their democracy. His 1943 painting *Geopoliticus Child Watching the Birth of the New Man* depicts Earth in the shape of an egg. Tearing away the eggshell is an adult man who emerges from the North American continent. Europe, on the other hand, is portrayed by the artist as a very minor landmass. Dalí's message was clear: The Americans would rise as leaders from the ashes of World War II.

Dalí's countryman, Miró, also lived in France during the Spanish Civil War and, like Dalí, was forced to flee France as war in Europe grew near. He could not return to Spain, where Franco would have had him arrested. Instead, he hid on the island of Majorca off the coast of Spain until he could safely return to France after World War II.

Escaping the War

As the Nazis gained power and swept through Europe, they targeted the Surrealist artists. Hitler—a failed artist himself—disliked abstract art and directed the Nazi party to conduct public burnings of abstract works. Masson found himself the target of Nazi wrath. He escaped and made his way to the United States, where his artwork was seized at the U.S. Customs station by agents who regarded it as obscene. The customs agents ripped up Masson's paintings as the artist looked on in horror.

Masson spent the war in Connecticut and continued to paint and used his art to denounce the Nazi regime. His 1942 painting *There Is No Finished World* was intended as an anti-war statement. It depicts a fight between two abstract figures while a third figure, a minotaur—a man with a bull's head—watches from the side. In Masson's mind, the minotaur represented death.

While Masson managed to escape the Nazis, Ernst was not so lucky. Arrested in 1939, Ernst spent two years in Camp des Milles, a labor camp where he was put to work making bricks. In the camp, he met Hans Bellmer, also a Surrealist. While in detention, Bellmer painted a portrait of Ernst—it depicts the sullen artist, his face composed of bricks against a stark black background.

Ernst was released in 1941 and made his way to America, where he used his art to depict Europe in the struggles of warfare. Among these paintings is *Europe After the Rain II* from 1942, which shows a soldier with the head of a bird wading through a field of ruins and desolation. For the painting, Ernst used the decalcomania technique, which enhanced the feeling he had tried to convey of a decaying countryside. Faerna wrote, "This method proved ideal for Ernst's prefiguration of the desolation and death that would descend over Europe at the conclusion of the war."[60] Another Ernst painting, *The Temptation of St. Anthony*, which the artist painted in 1945, shows hideous beasts tearing at the flesh of St. Anthony. The background of this chaotic scene is dominated by a serene European landscape.

Ernst spent the early years of the war in New York where he met Tanning, the woman he left his wife, Peggy Guggenheim, for. In 1946, Ernst and Tanning settled in Sedona, Arizona.

They married this same year after Ernst divorced his wife. Ernst was completely taken with his new home. His neighbors often saw the German Surrealist clad in blue jeans as he hiked among the mesas and canyons of the Sedona landscape. Ernst lived in Sedona until 1953, when he returned to Paris. He told his friends that there were only two places in the world where he would want to live; one was Paris, and the other was Sedona.

As for Dalí, he returned to Spain in 1949 where he was welcomed home as a hero by Franco. Dalí's longing to return to Spain was evidently a much greater force in his life than the memory of his friend Lorca, who had been murdered on Franco's orders. Indeed, Dalí congratulated the dictator for bringing order to the country and wiping out the subversive elements. "I have reached the conclusion," he said, "that (Franco) is a saint."[61] Dalí's embrace of the Fascist dictator further infuriated Breton and the other leaders of the Surrealist movement; however, Dalí brushed off their criticisms. He had always regarded himself as the only true Surrealist and, therefore, did not need the friendship or support of other artists.

Dalí lived the rest of his life near his boyhood home in the Catalonia region of Spain, although he often traveled and enjoyed the busy nightlife of New York and other big cities. He painted when the mood inspired him, although his output declined as he grew older. His work also became far less political; still, he had no regrets. In 1953, Dalí summed

Max Ernst is shown here standing among several of his paintings in his studio.

Camp des Milles

The labor camp where Max Ernst was imprisoned for two years at the outset of World War II was known as Camp des Milles because it was located near a French village called Les Milles. At first, the camp was used to hold Germans who were living in France at the time of the Nazi invasion of that country. Later, the Nazis used Camp des Milles as a concentration camp, where French Jews and other victims of the Third Reich were held before their deportation to Auschwitz and other death camps.

Ironically, when he was arrested by the French police, Ernst was working on a Surrealist landscape titled *A Moment of Calm*. The 1939 painting depicts a colorful landscape under a serene sky.

Camp des Milles included a brick factory, where Ernst was put to work. His cellmate was Hans Bellmer, another German Surrealist artist. Although Ernst won his release from custody, Bellmer remained imprisoned for the duration of the war. Bellmer survived the war, returned to Paris, and went on to create Surrealist drawings and photographs.

up his life: "Every morning upon awakening," he said, "I experience a supreme pleasure: that of being Salvador Dalí, and I ask myself, wonderstruck, what [amazing] thing will he do today, this Salvador Dalí."[62]

Debord, Rumney, and the Situationists

While Dalí relaxed in Catalonia and stayed out of Spanish politics, across the Mediterranean Sea in the Italian village of Cosio di Arroscia, a small group of intellectuals, political agitators, and artists met in 1957 to form a new group, which they named Situationist International. They embraced Marxism, but their philosophy was based on much more than just Socialist ideology. They believed that politicians and industrialists had caused wars, forced people to live in poverty, and allowed crime to take over the streets. They also believed that the ideas of truly creative people had been stifled. They decided that art—and in particular, Surrealist art—should be a guiding force in society. To promote social change, they advocated labor strikes, riots, and other radical actions.

Situationism—as the movement was called—never really caught on. Over the years, the situationists fought among themselves and divided into various subgroups; however, they remained heavily influenced by Surrealism. Their leader, Guy Debord, was a devoted student of Breton's writings. One of the founding members of Situationist International was the English Surrealist artist Ralph Rumney, who was the son-in-law of Guggenheim. Rumney believed that cities could be redesigned through automatism—that planners could wander through a city designing streets, bridges, buildings, fountains, sidewalks, and other urban features wherever their imaginations took them. Rumney applied his theory to a redesign for Venice, Italy, and proposed that the city's famous canals be dyed bright green. "Situationism," Rumney described, was "artistic, political and philosophical games which provoked an extreme reaction, and which put you back in touch with real experience, real life."[63]

Rumney's 1957 Surrealist painting *The Change* once hung in London's famed Tate Gallery. The colorful abstract work shows stabs of paint over a grid of black streaks. According to the Tate's catalog, "The combination of chance marks and the ordering device of a grid has been interpreted as a visual metaphor for the interaction of the subconscious and conscious, as well as the spiritual and material."[64]

Rumney was welcomed into Surrealist circles after marrying Guggenheim's daughter, Pegeen. When Pegeen took her own life in 1967 in the couple's Paris home, her mother accused Rumney of encouraging the suicide. Rumney's former mother-in-law had him trailed by detectives, which eventually forced him to flee to London, where he arrived penniless. He later took a job as a telephone operator and married Debord's first wife, Michèle Bernstein, who was a dedicated situationist. They eventually divorced but remained close friends. In Rumney's later years, he painted only sporadically, dying of cancer in 2002.

Even the situationists, whose movement he helped found, abandoned him. In 1958, just a few months after the movement was established in Italy, Rumney received a letter from Debord kicking him out because he missed a deadline for submitting an article to the movement's journal. The letter said, "Of course we like you a lot, but you can understand that we don't make a habit of endlessly prolonging negligence in certain affairs, in which you, like us, have chosen to be involved."[65]

Paris Student Riots of 1968

As bizarre as their ideas may have seemed, the situationists nearly had a chance to test their theories. In 1968, widespread student rioting and labor strikes broke out in Paris. Leftist students occupied La Sorbonne, which was a university in Paris. During the uprising, the walls of the university were covered with such situationist-inspired slogans as "Abolish Class Society," "Terminate the University," and "Occupy the Factories."[66] For days, anarchy ruled the streets of Paris. For a brief period, it appeared as though the French government would fall, providing the situationists with the surreal society they had long wanted.

Shown here are French rioters in Montparnasse in 1968.

Several students and situationists used
art to protest views they did not support.

French authorities soon contained the uprising and returned calm to the city. To appease the labor unions, French industrialists agreed to pay higher wages to the workers. As for the students, without the backing of the labor unions, their dreams of forcing a Socialist take-over of the government were prevented. Still painting in 1968, Miró honored the situationist cause by producing the surrealist painting *May 1968*, which shows splashes and drips of black paint, colorful splotches, stark black lines, and handprints—all depicting the chaos and ultimate downfall of the movement. Art curator Matthew Gale explained Miró's reaction and tribute to the protests through this painting:

It captures the mixture of energy and celebration. The bright colours are urgent but the black appears to have been hurled at the canvas. The hand-print is a sign that goes back to the pre-historic painters marking their presence in the caves of Lascaux and Altamira. They state simply: "I am here" … this may be read as solidarity.[67]

Through making their art, the Surrealists substantially impacted people's views during World War II and the Spanish Civil War. In tense times, many of these artists inspired those opposed to Fascism. While many of their art pieces represented the traumatic outcomes of the wars happening at the time, some of them also embodied the hope for a better tomorrow.

CHAPTER FIVE

Modern Surrealism

The original Surrealists created paintings, photographs, sculptures, and other works now commended as some of the most classic pieces of 20th century art. Only after several years have these works gained immense recognition and are now widely known to have inspired and influenced numerous modern artists. Prestigious art museums all over the world regularly host exhibits of Surrealist paintings, which are typically attended by thousands of people. During an exhibition, it is not unusual for visitors to spend several minutes in front of a painting by Dalí trying to figure out exactly what the artist was thinking—or more appropriately, dreaming—when he envisioned the image.

Once those visitors leave the museums, they may not find the work by Dalí and the other Surrealists that much different from what they see in their everyday lives. Popular culture of today, including TV commercials, movies, music videos, and photography, is full of Surrealist images. While these images may be updated for modern times, the roads taken by artists to reveal the bizarre ideas and concepts behind the art remain the same.

Nissan Micra Commercial

TV commercials have, in fact, become a place where Surrealist directors can display their talents. For example, when the Nissan car company planned an advertising campaign for a new model, the Micra, it turned to American film director David Lynch to develop a TV commercial that would make the vehicle appeal to young drivers with a taste for the offbeat. Lynch responded by producing a commercial showing the Micra cruising down a rain-splashed city street in Paris. In the ad, the sky is blue-black, but the buildings that line the street are brightly lit. In one of the buildings, a woman with red hair watches as the car cruises by. Finally, overhead, a gigantic pair of hovering blue lips speak a few indecipherable words. In fact, the words spill forth in text from the lips as they are spoken.

Nissan's TV commercial oozes Surrealism, from the blue-black sky to the red hair of the woman to the blue lips suspended in space. After all, Ray suspended red lips over a French landscape in his 1934 painting *Observatory Time—The Lovers*, and many Surrealist artists have added words in text to their paintings, including Grosz's 1920 painting *Republican Automatons*, which shows indecipherable words spilling forth from the empty head of his robot.

David Lynch Films

The cinema has always served as an appropriate home for Surrealism. When Nissan decided it needed the touch of a Surrealist for its Micra commercial, it chose the right director in Lynch. Many of his movies and his TV series *Twin Peaks* have included Surrealist images. Among his films is the creepy 1986 thriller *Blue Velvet*, which opens with slimy beetles grappling with one another beneath the calmness of a manicured lawn; a few minutes later,

Jeffrey Beaumont, played by actor Kyle MacLachlan, discovers a severed human ear in a field. Lynch also directed the 1997 film *Lost Highway*, a bizarre film with two intersecting stories: one following jazz musician Fred Madison (played by Bill Pullman), who is accused of his wife's murder, and another following the story of mechanic Pete Dayton (played by Balthazar Getty), who has been manipulated into an affair by a woman who is cheating on her gangster boyfriend. The film includes the sudden appearance of a house burning in a desert. In another chilling scene, Madison encounters a strange man who says he is at Madison's house—even though the man is standing in front of him, with an eerie grin, during the conversation. Madison calls his house, and the man answers. Writer Wess Haubrich sums up the film: "*Lost Highway* is … not just [a] sleek … noir but a moral homily [lecture] on how jealousy festers … that is couched in the devices of surrealism and the theories of deviant psychology."[68]

Lynch, along with other film directors such as Terry Gilliam, David Cronenberg, Alejandro González Iñárritu, and Spike Jonze—whose real name is Adam Spiegel—are regarded as the top Surrealist directors working in American cinema today. Although Lynch has concentrated on dark mysteries and Cronenberg is best known for his horror stories, Surrealist cinema can also be light and funny. Gilliam has made a number of comedies—his 1998 film *Fear and Loathing in Las Vegas* features

David Lynch is known for his use of Surrealist elements in his projects.

a scene in a casino bar populated by lizards sipping cocktails—while Jonze directed the bizarre 1999 film *Being John Malkovich*. The film, written by Charlie Kaufman and starring John Cusack, tells the story of a puppeteer who finds a hidden door that allows him to enter the brain of the film and theater actor John Malkovich. In the film's most surreal scene, Malkovich discovers the door and enters his own brain. Looking out through his own eyes, Malkovich sees a surreal Malkovichian world: Everyone—men, women, and children—has his head, the only words anyone speaks are "Malkovich," and the only words printed in books, newspapers, restaurant menus, and so on are "Malkovich."

Summing up the work of cinema's modern surrealists, *The Times* film critic Ian Johns wrote:

Lynch, like Terry Gilliam and David Cronenberg, is a rare breed of filmmaker with Surrealist tendencies. His brand of suburban surreal in Blue Velvet *spawned a thousand crazed TV neighborhoods ... And Charlie Kaufman, author of* Being John Malkovich, *in which puppeteer John Cusack finds a portal into the actor's brain, is developing a casual Surrealism that delights a mainstream audience bored by effects-laden extravaganzas that can turn any object into surreal life.*[69]

Two films from Iñárritu that displayed Surrealist imagery included 2014's *Birdman* and 2015's *The Revenant*. In *Birdman*, actor Michael Keaton stars as washed-up movie star Riggan Thomson, who previously became famous for playing the role of a superhero named Birdman. During the film, Thomson is tormented by the internal voice of Birdman. In an attempt to become relevant in the acting world again, Thomson stages a Broadway adaptation of Raymond Carver's *What We Talk About When We Talk About Love*. Some scenes in the film include Thomson levitating, performing telekinesis (the alleged ability to move things with one's mind without touching the item), and diving off a New York City building and flying through the air. In *The Revenant,* a frontiersman named Hugh Glass (played by Leonardo DiCaprio), who is on a fur trading expedition, fights for survival after being attacked by a grizzly bear and abandoned by his hunting team. In this film, the surreal images are seen in several dreamlike sequences— one where Glass's wife is floating horizontally in a field and another in which his son turns into a tree.

French Surrealist Cinema

Surrealist filmmaking dates back at least to 1928, when Dalí and the Spanish-born director Luis Buñuel collaborated on a number of short films. One of the films they made together, *Un Chien Andalou* (in English, *An Andalusian Dog*), included several graphic scenes. Two years later, Dalí and Buñuel collaborated again on a full-length film, *L'Âge*

Alejandro González Iñárritu's film **The Revenant** contains Surrealist imagery.

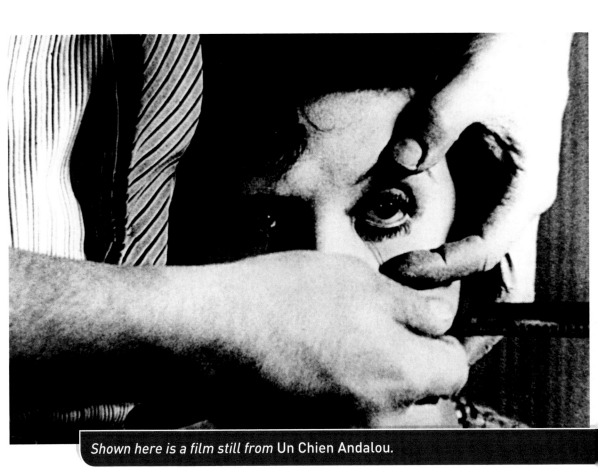

Shown here is a film still from **Un Chien Andalou.**

d'Or (in English, *The Golden Age*), which opens with a brief documentary about scorpions—and how their stings could be deadly—and then morphs into a story about a relationship between two people. The film includes scenes that Catholic leaders in France regarded as blasphemous. As a result, many theater owners refused to show the film. Cinema owners brave enough to screen the film often saw their theaters vandalized by rioters.

During the filming, Dalí and Buñuel had a falling out. The controversy over *L'Âge d'Or* finished—at least temporarily—both of their careers in French cinema, although Dalí continued to dabble in filmmaking from time to time. In 1945, he designed the dream sequence that British director Alfred Hitchcock filmed for his murder mystery *Spellbound*. That same year, Dalí collaborated with American animation mogul Walt Disney on the production of a 6-minute cartoon titled *Destino*. Set to Spanish music written by Mexican songwriter Armando Domínguez and sung by Dora Luz, the cartoon has no plot. It simply follows a young ballerina as she travels through a dreamy landscape dominated by creatures and images one would expect to see in a Dalí painting. The cartoon was not released until 2003—long after the deaths of Disney and Dalí—when Disney's heirs resurrected the long-forgotten Surrealist cartoon and issued it in a DVD version.

Meanwhile, the torch for French cinematic Surrealism was carried by Jean Cocteau, who also directed theater and ballet. In addition to a version of *Beauty and the Beast*, Cocteau directed *Orphée* in 1950, which was an updated version of the Greek mythological story *Orpheus*. The film followed Orphée's attempt to rescue his wife from the underworld. Cocteau included many Surrealist images: His characters walked through mirrors, messengers from the underworld were dressed as leather-clad motorcyclists, and the underworld itself was depicted as the bombed-out buildings of France left behind by World War II. By including such diverse images—some taken from real life, some make-believe—Cocteau fulfilled the Surrealist's challenge of combining the real with the unreal.

As for Buñuel, after his dispute with Dalí, he left France and emigrated to Mexico, where he made mainstream movies and became a citizen. Following World War II, Buñuel's interest in Surrealist cinema reemerged. In 1950, he directed the Mexican film *Los Olvidados* (in English, *The Young and the Damned*). The film tells the story of poor youths struggling to survive in Mexico; its Surrealist images include a

Hiro Murai

Tokyo-born filmmaker Hiro Murai is known for incorporating Surrealist imagery in the music videos he creates. Some of the artists he has worked with include Childish Gambino (otherwise known as Donald Glover), St. Vincent, Flying Lotus, and Queens of the Stone Age. He also has directed several episodes of Glover's comedy-drama television series *Atlanta*.

Several of the music videos Murai has directed for Glover include visual symbolism, which hints at underlying messages deep within the music. Glover's video "This Is America," which Murai directed, was viewed more than 10 million times within the first 24 hours after it was released in 2018. The video contains numerous symbols that have been analyzed by several critics. For example, at the beginning of the video, Glover is seen shooting a man playing a guitar with a bag over his head. Later on, he also shoots an entire gospel choir, which seems to be a reference to the 2015 Charleston, South Carolina, shooting of nine African American churchgoers by Dylann Roof. After each shooting he states, "This is America," and starts dancing with a group of schoolchildren in uniforms. Each time the group dances in the video, there are chaotic scenes unfolding in the background; however, the dancing initially distracts the viewer from these scenes. Aida Amoako from *The Atlantic* explained why the video is captivating and also disturbing at the same time:

The shooting itself is shocking, but so is that fact that Glover carries on dancing as if nothing happened.

An internal struggle begins in the viewer's body, which is pulled between joy and horror. Just as the video questions how we can dance when there is pandemonium all around, the audience struggles with whether to continue moving, too, after witnessing such brutality, especially after Glover shoots an entire choir of gospel singers.[1]

The video is a commentary on the topics of gun violence and racism in the United States. While the scenes in the video are fictional and shocking, they imitate real scenarios in the modern world.

Hiro Murai uses Surrealist concepts in the music videos and television episodes he directs.

1. Aida Amoako, "Why the Dancing Makes 'This Is America' So Uncomfortable to Watch," *The Atlantic*, May 8, 2018. www.theatlantic.com/entertainment/archive/2018/05/this-is-america-childish-gambino-donald-glover-kinesthetic-empathy-dance/559928/.

scene where a boy throws an egg at the camera lens as well as a dream sequence shot in slow motion. He returned to French cinema in 1972, when he directed his greatest triumph, *Le Charme Discret de la Bourgeoisie* (in English, *The Discreet Charm of the Bourgeoisie*), which won the Academy Award for Best Foreign Language Film in 1973. "Bourgeoisie" is a French term for the middle class; Karl Marx—whose philosophy has inspired generations of Surrealists—regarded the bourgeoisie as an enemy of the working class. Certainly, Buñuel did not intend for the film to shed a positive light on middle-class life.

Buñuel's film contains a confusing series of surreal scenes: diners meeting at a restaurant where a funeral is taking place, soldiers arriving at the restaurant for dinner, theatergoers watching the action of the movie unfold on a stage, and various dream sequences, among others. The characters accept all these features and events as though they are natural, everyday occurrences. Peter Bradshaw, film critic at *The Guardian*, wrote of the film,

The surrealist and anthropologist in Buñuel was fascinated by the ritual of the dinner party: without a host, this social event resembles humanity frantically inventing intricate rules for itself in the absence of God. It is still superbly disturbing when everyone assembles around a dinner table in an unfamiliar house and *then, when one wall suddenly moves away, they discover themselves to be on stage in a blaze of unnatural light, inspected by an auditorium full of frowning theatregoers.*[70]

Surreal Music Videos

There is no question that commercials and films are outlets for Surrealist directors. Another important platform for contemporary Surrealism is the music video. Indeed, if Surrealism has found a home in TV advertising and in the cinema, it has also flourished on YouTube and television networks that feature music videos.

Anybody who tunes to these channels is likely to see singers and dancers performing against backdrops of barren deserts, tropical seascapes, bizarre alien planets, and abstract backgrounds designed to appeal to the weird tastes of the viewers. In many cases, the little dramas played out in the videos appear to have nothing to do with the stories told in the lyrics of the songs.

Jonze has directed dozens of music videos. Among the performers who have been featured in his videos are such diverse singers as hip-hop stars Ludacris, Fatboy Slim, and The Notorious B.I.G.; Sean Lennon, the son of the late Beatle John Lennon; and the alternative rock star Björk. Jonze directed the video for Björk's 1995 song "It's Oh So Quiet." The video shows the Icelandic singer strolling down the center of a small American town, where she is joined by a number of elderly women twirling umbrellas, a dancing mailbox, and a flash mob in the street consisting of a diverse group of people.

When former *Boston Globe* film critic Wesley Morris saw the 2004 video for "Y Control" that Jonze directed for the dance-punk group Yeah Yeah Yeahs, he was immediately reminded of the film *Un Chien Andalou* because the video contains disturbing imagery. Morris wrote, "Singer Karen O and her band appear to be performing at the most exuberantly sick 10-year-old birthday party ever. It's in part a tribute to Luis Buñuel's 1929 silent 'Un Chien Andalou.' The setting is a dank parking garage, and Jonze's lighting is cheap horror-movie stuff that catches a dozen or so kids wilding out."[71]

The Computer's Influence on Surrealism

Despite Surrealism's influence on movies, TV commercials, and music videos, the genre has always been an art form most commonly seen on the walls of galleries. Although the great artists of Surrealism have now been dead for decades, the genre has been kept alive by many contemporary painters and photographers.

One of the top Surrealists working today is fashion photographer David LaChapelle, who was recognized by Andy Warhol early in his career. He is most well known for taking photographs for *Interview* magazine and directing music videos for artists such as Florence + The Machine, Britney Spears, Elton John, and Christina Aguilera, among others.

In 2006, *American Photo* magazine featured a retrospective of his work and included several of his most familiar images on its pages. Among them were his 1998 image *Madonna in Bombay in New York*, featuring the pop singer Madonna curled up in a giant purple hand, which is itself set up in a dingy public lavatory, and *Elton John at Home*, shot in 1997 and featuring singer Elton John standing on a piano decorated with leopard spots, surrounded by stuffed leopards in a room whose walls are adorned with huge depictions of bananas and cherries. Another image in the retrospective was *Parasol*, a fashion photo published in *Italian Vogue* in 2005. The shot features a model in a flowing white gown, carrying a torn umbrella and walking past a scene of devastation in which a home has been torn in two with debris scattered on the front lawn.

Like most photographers working today, LaChapelle creates pictures through digital imaging, which has created many opportunities for the Surrealist artist. Anyone with access to a computer, internet, a digital camera, and a photo-editing program can become a Surrealist. However, he cautions young photographers to be wary of the process, suggesting that no amount of manipulation on the computer can improve a poor photograph. "The computer is slave to the camera, because without a good

Surrealist Collage Art

Several artists today credit early Surrealists as strong influences. Eugenia Loli and Bryan Olson, who create surreal collages, make each one with a mixture of images that come together to make one dreamlike image.

Loli, who is originally from Greece but now resides in California, started out as a computer programmer and tech journalist. In 2012, she began making collages. In her opinion, collage art is an accessible medium of art

Bryan Olson uses Surrealist imagery within his collages, such as the work shown here..

1. Bryan Olson, interview by author, May 28, 2018.
2. Eugenia Loli, interview by author, May 15, 2018.

photograph all the technology in the world doesn't take a good picture. You have to have a good photograph to begin with."[72] The 21st century Surrealist artist can start by taking their own digital pictures. Then, with millions of images available on the internet, the artist can find many weird and bizarre images to download. Using a photo-editing program, such as Adobe Photoshop, these shots of the familiar and unfamiliar can be chopped up and refashioned into Surrealist art. It is likely that Surrealism's first photographer, Ray, would approve of this technique. He once said, "I never think about art, and I don't think the old masters ever thought they were creating art.

that does not require training. For her art, she mostly uses vintage images from the 1950s.

Olson, who resides in Portland, Oregon, is originally from Chicago, Illinois. He began drawing when he was young, but his only art training came from art classes during his freshman and sophomore years of high school. In his mid-20s, he got into creating collage art.

To find materials for his collages, Olson regularly spends a lot of time in thrift stores and used bookstores looking through the pages of old books and magazines for imagery that stands out to him. After he finds a batch of images, he makes intricate cuts with scissors or an X-Acto knife to extract the parts of the images he wants to use and then pieces the final image together. Each collage takes a couple of hours to create if he has all the pieces; it can take months if he needs to search for a specific missing piece.

Loli and Olson have been inspired by the work of several modern artists, such as Kazumasa Nagai, Robert Beatty, Cur3es, David Delruelle, and Jeffrey Meyer. However, Magritte is one artist who has had a profound influence on both of them.

While all artists may have a different definition of what Surrealism means to them, Loli and Olson both agree that it is similar to what most may see in their dreams. "Surrealistic art to me is art that doesn't follow any rules," Olson said. "It's like when you're dreaming, your thoughts are fluid and unpredictable."[1] According to Loli, to achieve a Surrealist work, it depends on a person's "ability to portray altered states of consciousness. Surrealism is dream symbolism, and only one step from full-on psychedelic work."[2]

They had to express the spirit of their times. They would start to invent. And those were the Surrealists of their time. Every period had its Surrealists."[73]

Pop Surrealist Movement

Of course, some Surrealists prefer to create their art the way that Dalí, Ernst, and Magritte created Surrealism— with paintbrushes and canvases. Many major cities feature at least one gallery that specializes in Surrealist art produced by contemporary painters. So far, none of these artists have attained the fame, wealth, and recognition of the original Surrealists; nevertheless, a small and dedicated segment of the art-loving community maintains a fascination with the Surrealist school of thought. There is no question that today's Surrealist artists are producing some truly bizarre images that carry on the work of the original Surrealist masters.

Today's Surrealist artists have a new name for their genre: They call it "Pop Surrealism." It is also known as "lowbrow" art, but many Pop Surrealists regard that as a derogatory term. Pop Surrealist art can be found in the pages of the quarterly journal *Juxtapoz*, a publication founded in 1994 by California artist Robert Williams. Pop Surrealism often carries dark messages. While the characters are generally drawn as cartoonish figures, the messages and images are just as bizarre as those painted by Dalí, who serves as an icon to the movement. "When we started *Juxtapoz*, we wanted a place for the outlaw art that wasn't being seen anywhere,"[74] Williams said.

Admiration for the Pioneers

While the Pop Surrealists develop their unique brand of Surrealism, the paintings, photographs, films, and other works produced by the original Surrealist artists from the 1920s and 1930s continue to draw large audiences. In recent years, major Surrealist shows featuring the works of Dalí, Ray, Ernst, and the other founders of the movement have been held at major museums in many large American cities. In 2005, an exhibition of Dalí's paintings at the Philadelphia

Museum of Art drew tens of thousands of visitors. The curators of the show dedicated a large portion of the museum to the late Spanish Surrealist's work. More than 200 of his paintings were exhibited. In fact, the concrete steps to the museum were decorated with a huge and colorful portrait of Dalí plastered right into the concrete surface, spanning thousands of square feet. The late Anne d'Harnoncourt, former director of the museum, said, "Dalí is one of the best-known artists of all time and yet, 16 years after his death and despite such remarkable public recognition, his achievement has yet to be fully understood … This exhibition will provide a splendid opportunity for scholars, artists, and visitors to encounter a complete and complex picture of the artist's [works]."[75]

The Dalí show proved to be highly successful; in fact, the museum was forced to extend the show by two weeks because of all the requests for tickets. Judging by the popularity of the exhibition, it is clear that the work of Dalí and his contemporaries still commands a dedicated audience. A large number of people have observed original Surrealist art work up close and have found themselves as confused and as captivated by the movement as the first audiences were more than three-quarters of a century ago.

Surrealism birthed a number of other art movements, including Abstract Expressionism, Pop Art, situationism, Pop Surrealism, and Afro-Surrealism, which is a cultural response to mainstream Surrealism to reflect the experiences of people of color. It even influenced music and activism, such as the feminist movement, civil rights movement, and the punk rock movement, all of which occurred in the 1960s and 1970s. All these movements were about reaching outside of the norms of society and displaying unconventional views. Surrealism was about projecting one's innermost thoughts of the sub-conscious to create art with symbolic messages that represented the artist's feelings about particular issues regarding society and life. As artists have embraced the aspects of Surrealism in their works of art today, there has yet to be a singular Surrealist artist who has dazzled the masses as the original Surrealists did. However, Surrealism will surely continue to have a deep impact on current art movements and all future art.

Notes

Introduction: Defining Surrealism

1. Quoted in Sigmund Freud, *The Major Works of Sigmund Freud*. Chicago, IL: University of Chicago, 1952, p. 168.
2. Jennifer Mundy, ed., *Surrealism: Desire Unbound*. Princeton, NJ: Princeton University Press, 2001, p. 12.
3. Quoted in Jonathan Lear, *Freud*. Oxford, UK: Routledge, 2015, p. 96.

Chapter One: Early Surrealism

4. Quoted in Hans Richter, *Dada: Art and Anti-Art*. New York, NY: Thames and Hudson, 1997, p. 37.
5. Alfred H. Barr Jr., *Cubism and Abstract Art*. Cambridge, MA: Harvard University Press, 1986, p. 78.
6. Otto Hahn, *Masson*. New York, NY: Harry N. Abrams, Inc., 1965, pp. 6–7.

7. Quoted in René Passeron, *Surrealism*. Paris, France: Pierre Terrail, 2001, p. 1,917.
8. Quoted in Anna Balakian, *André Breton: Magus of Surrealism*. New York, NY: Oxford University Press, 1971, p. 64.
9. André Breton, *Manifesto of Surrealism*, University of Alabama Department of Telecommunications and Film, accessed on June 11, 2018. www.tcf.ua.edu/Classes/Jbutler/T340/SurManifesto/ManifestoOfSurrealism.htm.
10. Breton, *Manifesto of Surrealism*.
11. Uwe M. Schneede, *Surrealism*. New York, NY: Harry N. Abrams, 1973, p. 62.
12. Tim Martin, *Essential Surrealists*, Bath, UK: Dempsey Parr, 1999. p. 79.
13. Carolyn Lanchner, *Joan Miró*. New York, NY: Museum of Modern Art, 1993, p. 33.
14. Quoted in Schneede, *Surrealism*, p. 76.

15. A. M. Hammacher, *Magritte*. New York, NY: Harry N. Abrams, 1985, p. 48.
16. Schneede, *Surrealism*, p. 104.
17. Quoted in Salvador Dalí, *The Secret Life of Salvador Dalí*. New York, NY: Dover Publications, 1993, p. 213.
18. Quoted in Schneede, *Surrealism*, p. 92.

Chapter Two: Essential Surrealists

19. Quoted in Paul Moorhouse, *Dali*. San Diego, CA: Thunder Bay, 1990, p. 15.
20. Quoted in C. W. E. Bigsby, *Dada and Surrealism*. London, UK: Routledge, 2018, p. 69.
21. Quoted in Tim McNeese, *Salvador Dali*. New York, NY: Chelsea House, 2006, p. 15.
22. Moorhouse, *Dali*, p. 92.
23. Robert Goff, *The Essential Salvador Dalí*. New York, NY: Harry N. Abrams, 1998, p. 57.
24. Quoted in John Russel, "Salvador Dalí, Pioneer Surrealist, Dies at 84," *New York Times*, 1989. www.nytimes.com/1989/01/24/obituaries/salvador-dali-pioneer-surrealist-dies-at-84.html.
25. Quoted in "Introduction," in *Salvador Dalí: Liquid Desire*, National Gallery of Victoria, accessed on June 7, 2018.
www.ngv.vic.gov.au/dali/salvador/resources/daliandsurrealism.pdf.
26. Ingrid Schaffner, *The Essential Man Ray*. New York, NY: Harry N. Abrams, 2003, p. 34.
27. Quoted in *American Masters*, "Man Ray: Prophet of the Avant-Garde," PBS, September 17, 2005. www.pbs.org/wnet/americanmasters/man-ray-prophet-of-the-avant-garde/510/.
28. Marina Vanci-Perahim, *Man Ray*. New York, NY: Harry N. Abrams, 1998, p. 56.
29. Schaffner, *The Essential Man Ray*, p. 27.
30. David Sylvester, *Magritte: The Silence of the Word*. New York, NY: Harry N. Abrams, 1992, p. 296.
31. Bradley Collins Jr., "Psychoanalysis and Art History," *Art Journal*, Summer 1990, p. 182.
32. José María Faerna, *Ernst*. New York, NY: Harry N. Abrams, 1997, p. 21.
33. John Russell, *Max Ernst: Life and Work*. New York, NY: Harry N. Abrams, 1967, p. 133.
34. Jacques Lassaigne, *Miró*. Paris, France: Editions d'Art, 1963, p. 40.
35. Lassaigne, *Miró*, p. 41.
36. Schneede, *Surrealism*, p. 86.

Chapter Three: Artists Influenced by Surrealists

37. Schneede, *Surrealism*, p. 51.
38. "Art: Marvelous and Fantastic," *TIME*, December 14, 1936. content.time. com/time/subscriber/ article/0,33009,757163,00. html.
39. Quoted in Steven W. Naifeh and Gregory White Smith, *Jackson Pollock: An American Saga*. New York, NY: Clarkson N. Potter, 1989, p. 417.
40. Quoted in Naifeh and Smith, *Jackson Pollock*, p. 419.
41. Quoted in Naifeh and Smith, *Jackson Pollock*, p. 454.
42. Schneede, *Surrealism*, p. 132.
43. Quoted in Mundy, *Surrealism: Desire Unbound*, p. 197.
44. Quoted in "Artists on Art: David Hare on Sunrise," Albright Knox Art Gallery, March 6, 2017. www.albrightknox.org/ blog/artists-art-david-hare-sunrise.
45. Quoted in Victor Bockris, *Warhol: The Biography*. Cambridge, MA: Da Capo Press, 2003, pp. 198–199.
46. Bruce H. Hinrich, "Chaos and Cosmos: The Search for Meaning in Modern Art," *Humanist*, March/April 1995, p. 22.
47. Quoted in Bob Colacello, *Holy Terror: Andy Warhol Close Up.* New York, NY: HarperCollins, 2014, p. 236.
48. Hayden Herrera, *Frida Kahlo: The Paintings*. New York, NY: Perennial, 1991, pp. 188–190.
49. Quoted in Mundy, *Surrealism: Desire Unbound*, p. 201.
50. Quoted in Anwen Crawford, "Leonora Carrington Rewrote the Surrealist Narrative for Women," *New Yorker*, May 22, 2017. www.newyorker. com/books/page-turner/ leonora-carrington-rewrote-the-surrealist-narrative-for-women.
51. Quoted in Farahnaz Zahidi, "Frida Kahlo's art: Ribbon around a bomb," *The Express Tribune*, November 9, 2014. tribune.com.pk/story/786794/ frida-kahlos-art-ribbon-around-a-bomb/.

Chapter Four: Art Advocating Social Change

52. André Breton, *Conversations: The Autobiography of Surrealism*. New York, NY: Paragon House, 1993, p. 97.
53. Bruce B. Lawrence and Aisha Karim, *On Violence*. Durham, NC: Duke University Press, 2007, p. 500.
54. Quoted in Manny Thain, "Real Enough," *Socialism Today*, October 2001.

www.socialismtoday.org/60/surrealism/html.

55. H. H. Arnason, Marla F. Prather, and Daniel Wheeler, *History of Modern Art*. New York, NY: Harry N. Abrams, 1998, p. 286.

56. Hammacher, *Magritte*, p. 86.

57. Quoted in Moorhouse, *Dali*, p. 82.

58. Quoted in Martin, *Essential Surrealists*, p. 136.

59. Moorhouse, *Dali*, p. 94.

60. Faerna, *Ernst*, p. 50.

61. Quoted in Richard Lacayo, "Dalí Goes to Rehab," *TIME*, February 21, 2005, p. 59.

62. Quoted in Stanley Meisler, "The Surreal World of Salvador Dalí," *Smithsonian*, April 2005. www.smithsonianmag.com/arts-culture/the-surreal-world-of-salvador-dali-78993324/.

63. Quoted in "Ralph Rumney," *Independent*, March 26, 2002. www.independent.co.uk/news/obituaries/ralph-rumney-9169665.html.

64. *"The Change,"* Tate Gallery, accessed on June 11, 2018. www.tate.org.uk/art/artworks/rumney-the-change-t05556.

65. Quoted in "Ralph Rumney," *The Times*, March 29, 2002.

66. Quoted in Situationist International Online, "Slogans to Be Spread Now by Every Means," Virginia Tech University, accessed on June 11, 2018. www.cddc.vt.edu/sionline/si/slogans.html.

67. Walter Erben, *Joan Miró: The Man and His Work*. Cologne, Germany: Benedikt Taschen, 1998, p. 208.

Chapter Five: Modern Surrealism

68. Wess Haubrich, "A Sexy, Sleek as a Stiletto Surrealist, Moral Homily: Lost Highway at 20 Years," The 405, May 11, 2017. www.thefourohfive.com/film/article/a-sexy-sleek-as-a-stiletto-surrealist-moral-homily-lost-highway-1997-at-20-years-149.

69. Ian Johns, "Here's One in the Eye," *The Times*, September 19, 2001.

70. Peter Bradshaw, "The Discreet Charm of the Bourgeoisie—Review," *The Guardian*, June 28, 2012. www.theguardian.com/film/2012/jun/28/discreet-charm-bourgeoisie-review.

71. Wesley Morris, "Now That's What I Call Video," *Boston Globe*, February 5, 2006. archive.boston.com/ae/movies/articles/2006/02/05/now_thats_what_i_call_video/.

72. Quoted in "David LaChapelle: Interview with One of Photography's Brightest Stars," designboom, accessed on June 11, 2018. www.designboom.com/eng/interview/lachapelle.html.

73. Quoted in *Morning Edition*, "Profile: New Surrealist Art

Exhibition at the Metropolitan Museum of Art in New York," National Public Radio, March 5, 2002.

74. Quoted in Doug Harvey, "Pictures from the Unibrow Revolution," L.A. *Weekly*, October 27, 2005. www.laweekly.com/news/ pictures-from-the-unibrow-revolution-2140978.

75. Quoted in "Salvador Dali: The Grand Master of Surrealism," USA *Today*, May 2005, p. 34.

For More Information

Books

Klingsöhr-Leroy, Cathrin. *Surrealism*. Cologne, Germany: Taschen, 2015.
     This book gives an introduction to Surrealism, the movement's artists,
     and 35 of their most important works. It also includes 30 photographs and
     a timeline.

Lowenstein, Adam. *Dreaming of Cinema: Spectatorship, Surrealism, and the Age
of Digital Media*. New York, NY: Columbia University Press, 2015.
     Various Surrealist artists are highlighted in this book as key influences
     on modern directors. Many of the films made in the 21st century are
     examined in this book that discusses how Surrealism has impacted the
     content and techniques presented in these films.

Parkinson, Gavin, ed. *Surrealism, Science Fiction and Comics*. Liverpool, UK:
Liverpool University Press, 2015.
     This is a guide to the links between Surrealism and science fiction and
     how this influenced the world of comics, told through 10 original essays.

Zalman, Sandra, and Gavin Parkinson. *Consuming Surrealism in American
Culture: Dissident Modernism*. Aldershot, UK: Ashgate Publishing, 2015.
     Zalman and Parkinson provide insight into the Surrealist movement's
     impact on American culture and how it was presented in museums and
     various art communities.

Websites

Gallery of Surrealism

www.surrealism.gallery/index.htm

> This website provides a list of Surrealist artists along with images of their artwork. Upcoming dates for galleries around the world displaying Surrealist artists' work is also included.

Juxtapoz

www.juxtapoz.com

> The quarterly journal of Pop Surrealism includes many images of Surrealist art created by contemporary artists. The website also includes a list of exhibitions and other events involving Pop Surrealism, articles on Pop Surrealism, reviews of recent work, and a page where readers can post their own art.

Salvador Dalí Museum

thedali.org

> The official website for the Dalí Museum in St. Petersburg, Florida, includes many resources for students studying the Spanish Surrealist, including a biography of Dalí, online videos featuring curators discussing Dalí's work, and instructions for students on how to make their own Dalí "characters," including his long-legged elephants and giraffes.

Surrealism Today

surrealismtoday.com/artists

> This blog gives young readers a fun look inside the world of contemporary Surrealism created by a diverse group of artists, which includes paintings, digital art, collage, sculpture, and video.

Index

Picture Credits

Cover (screen image) Rawpixel.com/Shutterstock.com; cover (main image) Caron Badkin/Shutterstock.com; pp. 1, 3, 4, 6, 11, 27, 46, 64, 78, 92, 97, 99, 103, 104 (big paint swatch) Lunarus/Shutterstock.com; p. 7 TIZIANA FABI/AFP/Getty Images; p. 8 Courtesy of the Library of Congress; p. 13 Allan Grant/The LIFE Picture Collection/Getty Images; p. 14 Dan Kitwood/Getty Images; pp. 14, 18, 30, 40, 44, 50, 54, 57, 67, 74, 85, 88 (paint caption background) Jaroslav Machacek/Shutterstock.com; p. 16 Fine Art Images/Heritage Images/Getty Images; p. 18 ERIC CABANIS/AFP/Getty Images; p. 20 Roger Viollet Collection/Getty Images; p. 23 Michael Ochs Archives/Getty Images; p. 25 KAMMERMAN/Gamma-Rapho via Getty Images; p. 29 Allan/Express/Getty Images; p. 30 Culture Club/Getty Images; pp. 32–33, 66–67 FRANCOIS GUILLOT/AFP/Getty Images; pp. 34–35 Michel Sima/RDA/Getty Images; pp. 38–39 LUIS ACOSTA/AFP/Getty Images; pp. 40–41 Stephen Chung/Alamy Stock Photo; pp. 42–43 Alain Dejean/Sygma via Getty Images; p. 44 Keystone-France/Gamma-Keystone via Getty Images; p. 47 Reporters Associes/Gamma Features via Getty Images; p. 50 Martha Holmes/The LIFE Picture Collection/Getty Images; p. 52 Michel Sima/Bridgeman Images; pp. 54–55, 57 Mario De Biasi/Mondadori Portfolio via Getty Images; pp. 58–59 Bettmann/Bettmann/Getty Images; pp. 64–65 Leon Neal/Getty Images; p. 71 Claude Huston/Pix Inc./The LIFE Images Collection/Getty Images; pp. 74–75 Central Press/Getty Images; p. 76 adrian gargett/Moment/Getty Images; p. 80 Jean-Christian BOURCART/Gamma-Rapho via Getty Images; p. 82 AF archive/Alamy Stock Photo; p. 83 Album/Art Resource, NY; p. 85 Kevin Winter/Getty Images; p. 88 Courtesy of Bryan Olson; back cover vector illustration/Shutterstock.com.

About the Author

Vanessa Oswald is an experienced freelance writer and editor who has written pieces for publications based in New York City and the Western New York area, which include *Resource* magazine, *The Public*, *Auxiliary* magazine, and *Niagara Gazette*. In her spare time, she enjoys dancing, traveling, reading, snowboarding, and attending live concerts.